PEOPLES OF THE MARITIMES

Acadians

Henri-Dominique Paratte

NIMBUS
PUBLISHING

Copyright © Henri-Dominique Paratte, 1998

Nimbus Publishing Limited
P.O 9301, Station A
3731 Mackintosh St.
Halifax, Nova Scotia B3K 5N5
(902) 455-4286

1st edition November 1991
2nd edition August 1998
Text editor: Douglas Beall
Cover painting by Tracadie artist Jean-Baptiste Comeau, better known as Komo.
Back cover photo: Martine Jacquot

CANADIAN CATALOGUING IN PUBLICATION DATA
Paratte, Henri-Dominique, 1950-
The Acadians
Rev. ed.
ISBN 1-55109-183-6
1. Acadians —History.   2. Acadians — Biography.
I. Title.
FC2041.P37 1998   971.5'004114   C98-950142-6
F1027.P37 1998

Nimbus Publishing acknowledges the support of the Canada Council and the Canadian Department of Heritage.

FOREWORD

The peoples of the Maritimes comprise in excess of seventy distinct and identifiable ethnic-cultural groups. Yet, only a few of these have their place in our history and our society well known and documented. The Peoples of the Maritimes series is an attempt to redress that imbalance by providing a well researched but readable collection of monographs for both the general and student reader.

The demographic face of Canada as a whole is changing rapidly as a result of national realities connected with the country's declining birth rate and the need for more immigrants to enhance economic growth. In this context, education and information are crucial for the promotion of harmonious social change.

The Maritimes has a rich diversity in its population, ranging all the way from the first nations and the pre-Confederation settlers to the later nation builders from all parts of the globe—more recently from Third World countries in increasing numbers. The literature on the Maritimes must keep pace with these changing times and challenges.

The Maritimes Peoples Project gratefully acknowledges the funding assistance provided for the development of this book by the Minister responsible for Multiculturalism, Government of Canada.

Bridglal Pachai, Ph.D.
General Editor

ACKNOWLEDGEMENTS

We are all the product of influences that go back to ancestors and parents. This book is dedicated first of all to my parents, Andrée Vigneron and Gabriel Paratte. They made me what I am, open to other cultures, but with a deep core of "Frenchness" which is neither racist nor parochial, and which my sons Igor and Thibault and my daughter Mélodie will, I hope, keep in a form adapted to another millennium and a presumably different Canada.

Many thanks to the lady who has weathered all the difficulties that writing a book such as this one, and many others, can bring to private life: my companion, fellow writer, journalist and photographer Martine L. Jacquot, who has become herself an active partner in the making of modern Acadian culture.

Having driven all over Acadian regions in the Maritimes for a quarter of a century, the list of all those who gave me greater insight into what being an Acadian in the last decades of the twentieth century could mean would be endless! While thanking all of them, I wish to acknowledge a special debt to Madame Antonine Maillet, one of the major writers of this century, who has always been the kindest person whenever our paths crossed; my fellow Acadian writers, who keep the flame alive, with special mention of Melvin Gallant, Herménégilde Chiasson and Claude LeBouthillier; the late Père Léger Comeau, the very soul of Acadie; Euclide Chiasson; the team of *Ven' d'est*; Paul Comeau; Barbara LeBlanc; the Fédération Acadienne de la Nouvelle-Écosse; Ronald Bourgeois, the Conseil Culturel Acadien de la Nouvelle-Écosse, the team of *Le Courrier*; Warren Perrin, Earlene Broussard and all those Cajuns who work with Codofil to bring French schools back to Louisiana, in an era when intercultural trade is increasingly important.

Many thanks also to all those I have met all over French Canada, from east to west: they all keep alive the flame of our culture and the pride we should derive from it, whatever difficulties its survival faces at times in a world where traditional values are of little help and where minorities continue to face intolerance and rejection. To all those who share the same ideal, in France, Louisiana, Quebec, Belgium, Switzerland, Senegal, and the Congo, thanks and best wishes for the future.

Henri-Dominique Paratte

CONTENTS

CHAPTER 1

From Whence They Came: The French Homeland and Acadie

> Historically, the francophone community can be linked with the very ancient culture of France ... As far as we French Canadians are concerned not only do we have a direct bloodline, we also have a genetic connection with it... I never forget that my ancestors, who came from France, lived at the same time as Molière. Afterwards, of course, we changed and we became Americans.
>
> -Antonine Maillet

Acadie (or Acadia), once a colony of France was the cradle of a new culture and a new people, the Acadians. Somehow the Acadians survived the many hardships they went through and have endured as a distinctive community. However different today from what it was in the past, Acadie still exists and grows as a francophone community.

At the time of the first Congrès Mondial Acadien in 1994, about 39,500 francophones were living in the "old Acadie" of Nova Scotia, where one citizen of every five could claim Acadian blood on one side or another. In New Brunswick, the "new Acadie," about 240,000 francophones kept the flame of their culture alive, and that flame was also kept burning on Prince Edward Island by its 6,000 francophones. In the Maritime region, Acadians are also today present on Saint-Pierre and Miquelon, belonging to France; in the Gaspé region and the Magdalen Islands, both part of Quebec; and on the island of Newfoundland, in the Port-au-Port area in particular. Acadians also live in every other province of Canada, every state of the United States and in several countries around the world.

The world cannot ignore the Acadians and Acadie, a country

without borders, without official statehood, but nevertheless a very real nation, Un pays, to which all Acadians have a sense of belonging. And one cannot fully understand the Acadians without some appreciation of their original European homeland and the French-speaking world to which they make a unique contribution.

I. France and Francophones Around the World Today

For Acadians, modern France is first of all a cultural power. It is also a major industrial power and a driving force behind the unification of Europe. Its high-tech and aeronautical industries, road construction technology, food processing plants and aluminum production are among the best today. Michelin is one of the three tire giants of the world and a major employer in Nova Scotia, and France has mastered nuclear technology for civilian and military purposes.

France is a country of culture, literature and ideas. Good food and good cheer, so dear to the early French settlers in the Maritimes, are still part of an animated way of life that fuses influences from southern and northern Europe. French taste and high fashion continue to create a standard of their own. Now crowded with more than 58 million people, France is a modern, industrialized and urban nation, quite in contrast to the sparsely populated, rural and peaceful Acadian shores of the Maritimes. This difference helps the Maritimes to attract tourists from France, who find in their "distant cousins" enough similarities to feel somewhat at home, and enough dissimilarities to feel in North America. In recent years, companies based in the Maritimes have started to offer tours with specific Acadian content, and several French magazines now present "Acadie" (the francophone parts of the Maritimes) to their readers when holiday season comes.

All regions of France have their own peculiar traits of language, culture and history, and Paris has for many centuries been an important national and international crossroads. But French is not only the language of France. It is also the language of the francophone communities in Belgium, the French-speaking cantons in Switzerland, and of Monaco, Andorra and the Val d'Aosta. It is also, of course, the language of Quebec—Montreal being the second largest francophone city in the world—and other French-speaking communities in Canadian provinces, from Ontario to British Columbia.

French Canadians in Quebec have been very supportive of the rise of Acadian nationalism since the 1880s and Quebec, whose beginnings are closely linked with those of Acadie, is conscious enough of its importance for other communities to have official representatives in many parts of the world, including the Maritimes, at Moncton.

French is also the language of many Franco-Americans. Six million U.S. citizens are of French descent, and even though a high percentage of them no longer speak French, most of those who do still wish to preserve it. French is also, because of France's former colonial empire, the language of many African countries, who retained it as an official language after independence. The Democratic Republic of Congo, formerly Zaire, with rich natural resources, is the second largest French-speaking country in the world, and Senegal has been on the forefront of the effort to build an international francophone community.

French is also the language of several islands in the Caribbean, some officially part of France such as the Antilles, (with a Black majority) and some officially independent (such as Haiti, which became in the nineteenth century the first Black Republic in the world). In the Caribbean, French often blends with Creoles, spoken languages based on a blending of French and African languages. French is the language of French Guyana, where France tests the European space program, and of French Polynesia, where France conducted nuclear tests. Although France retains few colonies today, French is spoken as a first language on four continents, and as a second language in many more countries, from Lebanon to Romania, from Egypt to Vietnam. From 1986, francophone countries have met at the highest level in the organization known as La Francophonie, with a summit of heads of state and/or government every two years. The 1999 summit will take place in Moncton, New Brunswick. The director of the organization is now Boutros Boutros-Ghali, former United Nations secretary general.

For Acadians, the French Caribbean has always been close. Boats have gone there and back since the early eighteenth century. For Acadians today, all francophone countries have become closer: Acadian boat engines are sold to Morocco, cultural exchanges with Belgium or Senegal are common, and this is bound to intensify with the rapid growth of planetary networks that is evident at the end of the twentieth century.

How many francophones live on earth today? About 400 million people according to recent francophone summits and, of these, about 125 million speak French most of the time and 70 million have French as their "mother tongue." These 70 million people, of which Acadians represent 300,000 to 400,000, will be 160 million in the year 2000. On five continents, about forty countries have French as a national or official language. French is one of the most important

Forum des Halles, Paris.

international languages (along with English and Spanish), one of the major languages used by Africans to communicate with the world, one of the official languages of Canada, and one of the essential languages in the new European Community. It is a language of diplomacy, the language of some of the major advances in politics and thought, and possibly the major language of modern culture in many fields of the arts. For the Maritimes, a francophone community is a major asset.

Badly bruised and largely ruined by the Second World War fought on its soil, which resulted in the reign of the two "superpowers" the USA and the former USSR, France has now once again become a major influence in world economy and politics, and the rising influence of francophones in North America and Africa has strengthened the French presence at the United Nations and elsewhere. To varying extents, all francophones, and particularly those for whom French is a mother tongue, partake of a rich, diverse and dynamic heritage.

Despite the fact that the source of all francophones is not France alone, but the European linguistic community of which it is part (which includes Belgium and Switzerland), France remains by far the most important country in the francophone world. Major distinctions can be made among francophones. Acadians are not "francophone" in the same way as the Senegalese or Lebanese. Acadians, like the majority of North American francophones, descend from a group of people who were moved or chose to move to a colony of France and took root there. Their "French" identity was not cast upon another identity, as it was for people the world over, from Africa to the Caribbean and Polynesia. Acadians were originally from specific provinces of France, and their language and culture is distinctive as a result.

II. The Rise of Modern France

The French who come to the Maritimes today come from a very different France than those who came at the time Acadie was founded. Although seventeenth-century France was a major European power, its territory was not as large or unified as it is today. All regions had major linguistic, cultural and economic differences. Although the kings of France had gradually gained power over feudal warlords in many regions after the thirteenth century, the system still required the king and his advisors to rely on diplomacy to ensure support by noblemen and princes to expand and defend the growing kingdom against foreign influences of all kinds, particularly against the threat of England, France's arch rival until the end of the nineteenth century.

The French have not forgotten that, during the Hundred Years War that raged from 1337 to 1453 and marked the end of the Middle Ages, England laid claim to its territory, even declaring the French king illegitimate in 1420. In the centre of Rouen stands today a memorial to Joan of Arc, a symbol of French unity not only because she defeated English armies and freed all of France, but because she was moved by a national fervour that represented the wishes of ordinary people, merchants and noblemen. With Joan of Arc came the notion of the King as the embodiment of a national will supported by divine choice.

By 1453, France was no longer simply a group of unconnected feudal regions, but a sovereign state. In the fifteenth century Louis XI, a cunning, brilliant and ruthless politician, expanded its territory, established roads, promoted trade fairs and created regulations for the whole kingdom. He also created the conditions necessary for a century of peace, which enabled peasants to produce more and eat better, towns to grow and trade and commerce to prosper. Incomes rose in rural areas, feudal control became less stringent; noblemen, at the time, could not work and did not pay taxes, which were shouldered largely by the peasants and the growing urban middle class.

HENRI-DOMINIQUE PARATTE

L'Académie Française, Paris.

SUZANNE GERRIOR

*Maison de l'Acadie,
La Chaussée, France.*

A general view of La Rochelle, France.

Paris then was small by today's standards but was the largest city in France, with 100,000 inhabitants, and already a major center for Europe.

Charles VIII, Louis XII and Francois I tried to conquer Italy during the fifteenth century. They did not achieve their military goal, but the influence of the Italian wars was obvious in the "Renaissance" movement in France. The castles along the Loire River, a region from which several Acadians and founders of Acadie, such as d'Aulnay, came, and the new art and poetry, now written in French as well as Latin, bore the mark of new influences. From 1534, following the Reformation, Protestants opposed a royal power solidly based on Catholicism. A massacre of Huguenots occurred during the night of Saint Bartholomew's Day in 1572 and until the Edict of Nantes in 1598, civil war raged and caused ruin throughout the land. Other wars followed, but France did not suffer as much as other countries, and the national territory increased at the end of the Thirty Years War in 1659.

HENRI-DOMINIQUE PARATTE

Charles de Menou d'Aulnay was a founder of Acadie.

Richelieu, the first minister of Louis XIII and strong man of the regime during the first half of the seventeenth century, unified the kingdom by considerably reducing noblemen's powers, a trend that Louis XIV, who acceded to the throne in 1661, reinforced, opening the way to a classical age in France and a powerful centralized government. Richelieu had created many new central institutions to promote French as the official language of law, letters and govern-ment documents. The institution everyone remembers is the Académie Française, which came under government supervision in 1635. Open to authors of French citizenship only, it is still closed in 1997 to all other authors writing in French, however famous they might be, and not very open to women.

Louis XIV, the "Sun King" gave his support to arts and letters, paving the way for French to become a universal language of the eighteenth century, the language of courts and diplomacy, major plays and brilliant essays.

Major explorations of Canada and Acadie took place during the reigns of Francois I and Henri IV; early settlement, the beginnings of the fur trade and the growth of New World fisheries came under Louis XIII; and the development of Canada, and other French colonies such as the French West Indies, took place under Louis XIV. The reign of Louis XV (1710-74) was marked by the loss of Canada and most of the French empire in North America to England, and by the Expulsion of the Acadians from their Maritime homelands after 1755. Under Louis XVI French military support helped the fledgling United States to obtain their freedom from the British.

A major event such as the American Revolution was known to Acadians. In 1782, rumours in the Maritimes were that a group of Americans, French naval officers and volunteers was planning to invade Canada and Nova Scotia. In 1778, Marion Arbuthnot, the lieutenant-governor of Nova Scotia, had greatly feared such an invasion and considered the Mi'kmaq and Acadians, once again, as potential traitors. However, although documents make it clear that Acadians generally felt closer to a United States supported by France than to their British masters, most of them remained neutral. Neither France nor the United States had indicated to them in any way that Acadie would be autonomous if the English were defeated. The France that helped the Americans was, after all, still one in which a subtle agreement between the king, his court, his ministers and the Catholic Church was the basis of political power. It was not yet a France of freedom, equality and brotherhood, but was still a France of privileges and entrenched powers. This was not the kind of system Acadians had grown to love in their own country of Acadie.

Louis XVI was the last king of France under the old regime of absolute powers. The Revolution of 1789, largely led by a prosperous middle class wishing to exercise political powers, and supported by most of the French people, marked the end of an era and the second advent of a modern republican system—the first being the American democracy, which had been influenced by French philosophies of the eighteenth century, like Montesquieu, Rousseau, or Diderot.

France in 1789 was a country of 26 million inhabitants and its territory was roughly the same as today. Most people, however, lived in regions that had such diverse identities and variations in tax laws, legal systems, economic development, religion and dialects that it was sometimes difficult to conceive of France as a unified national entity. Revolutionary governments, which lasted basically until 1802, had to fight wars on all fronts. They possessed an idea of liberty that no regime based on privileges could accept. Thus England, Spain, Austria, Prussia and Russia decided to get rid of the new French democracy. They were assisted by French noblemen furious at the loss of their privileges, and for whom any national ideal came second to the preservation of their own status. In western France a civil war raged for years.

The Republican government decided to ask priests to adhere to its principles or lose their right to engage in any activity. This led to the emigration of many brilliant, conservatively minded priests, who went to Britain where Catholic priests were tolerated but not particularly well received. From there some were authorized to go to Lower

SUZANNE GERRIOR

Town Hall, Poitiers, France.

Canada (now Quebec), but a smaller number went to the Acadian communities where priests were sorely needed. Priests at that time not only performed religious functions, but often acted as administrators, teachers and advisors on public matters.

One such priest was Jean-Mandé Sigogne, born in Beaulieu in 1763. Ordained in 1787, he refused to take the oath required by Republican authorities, and left for England where he worked as a labourer and a teacher for a few years. At that time, England had no desire to accept these "Republican" priests to work among the

Acadians who had come back to the Maritimes. Father Sigogne was sent to the Baie Sainte-Marie area in 1799. Although his Acadian flock may not have admired British institutions as much as he claimed, they came to respect him, and he showed an enormous amount of energy in building churches and developing an education system. He was named a justice of the peace and "leader" of the Clare Acadians by the British in 1810.

Acadians were mostly rural folk from regions of central western France (55 per cent of those who came to the Maritimes came from Poitou). They had an ingrained respect for the Catholic faith at a time when the rhythms of life were connected to religious festivals, fasting periods, and ceremonies. It is unlikely that they would have felt deep

MARTINE JACQUOT PHOTOS

The church at Abram-Village, P.E.I., left. Right: the column marking the first French site in North America, at Parris Island, SC.

sympathy with any movement that unduly oppressed the clergy, and there is indeed record of Acadians brought back to France who suffered prison and death in revolutionary times because of attachment to their faith. Also on record are the efforts of Father Le Loutre, who, after his captivity in England ended in 1763, helped to resettle some Acadian families in Brittany, particularly at Belle-Ile-en-Mer.

Acadians were not hostile to the Catholic Church, quite to the contrary. But some Acadians no doubt felt close, at the end of the eighteenth century, to ordinary French folk who stood up for their rights against the Church hierarchy, nobility and oppressive powers of all kinds. Acadians had been oppressed by a British colonial system fiercely opposed to their French and Catholic culture, they had been sometimes compelled to pay tithe to a highly conservative clergy that did not care much about their needs, and they had been forced to submit again and again to an "oath of allegiance" used against them at every turn. It is therefore not surprising that, however devout most of them may have been, a revolution in the land of their ancestors and companions triggered in some of them a feeling that struggling against injustice was not only possible but could also succeed and bring positive change. When Acadian star Edith Butler sings "Vive la République, vive la liberté," in concert today she is delivering a message that Acadians could respond to then as well as now.

The Revolution in France was quickly followed by the emergence of Napoleon I. Napoleon created institutions all over Europe, centralized France, reorganized education and fought wars all over Europe that left the country bloodless and exhausted in 1815. He also sold Louisiana to the United States for a pittance, giving away the last important chunk of the French continental empire in North America, and leaving Creole and Cajuns alike with the feeling that France had sold them to the Americans.

Napoleon I had given France administrative structures it would keep for a long time, despite the return of the Bourbon kings for short periods before the Second Republic was proclaimed in 1848. France was now an increasingly unified country and a major military and colonial power, and gradually became a country in which the large majority of the people lived in cities and towns. Although France remains to this day one of the major agricultural countries in Europe, it quickly became an important industrial power after the 1830s. As in other countries ruled by nineteenth-century paternalistic capitalism, where a small elite exerted financial and often political control over the majority, social unrest grew, with many workers' revolts, culminating in the ghastly massacres of the Paris commune in the 1870s. Little by little, however, progress was made to avoid clashes between the working class and the bourgeoisie.

After 1850 the empire of Napoleon III (a nephew of Napoleon I) gave France a more modern, industrial outlook and a major rail network. This last attempt at a system other than republican democracy vanished in the disaster of the first Franco-Prussian war in 1870. The very middle-class Third Republic, which lasted from 1870 to

1940, unified France at all levels, created a fully national public education system and added new colonial possessions. The world-famous Eiffel Tower, whose profile still dominates Paris, exemplified in 1900 the industrial, commercial and international aspirations of France.

Traditional bourgeois values and the "Belle Epoque" of the 1900s were shattered by the First World War, which was fought primarily on French soil and left the country exhausted by 1918, despite victory. The years that followed included the major failure of Western powers to curb Hitler's thirst for revenge. French people, now largely middle-class citizens, longed for social justice and peace. The socialist government in France, the Front Populaire, in 1936, despite its economic failures, marked a major change in the relationships among the various groups in society with progressive social legislation. It could not, however, stop a movement towards war, nor could it stop a right-wing fascination with a supposedly "redeeming" fascist ideology. Although it had the most powerful army and navy in Europe in 1939, France, betrayed by antiquated war plans and senile generals, went down in a few weeks before the German armies, leaving the soul of the nation crushed.

The infamous Vichy Regime, which slid into total collaboration with the Nazis, was quickly denounced by General Charles de Gaulle, whose "France Libre" forces gradually united all who wanted to see the entire nation free from tyranny. The Allied victory brought a coalition of parties to power, to quickly face the political intrigues of the weak Fourth Republic (1946-58). At a time when the country was essentially bandaging its many wounds, reconstructing, and adjusting to the new economic conditions of the 1950s, France also faced difficulties created by a powerful Communist party in a Europe dominated by American imperialism in the West and Russian imperialism in the East. It gradually lost its colonial empire, some-times through major military defeats, as in Indochina, and in Algeria, where French and Algerians fought one of the most vicious wars in modern times until 1961.

The return of de Gaulle to power, largely on the force of his self-proclaimed ability to resolve the Algerian crisis, opened the Fifth Republic in 1958 with a strong presidential regime that makes the president of France today one of the most powerful and influential people in the world. More democratic, youthful and urbanized than ever, France had to seek a balance between tradition and the chal-lenges of an increasingly global economy. The loss of its colonial empire changed the meaning of its military tradition. France was now able to act as a peacekeeper, particularly in African conflicts.

Charles de Gaulle created an international network of French-speaking countries and communities and gradually moved France away from direct U.S. influence. The man who dared to shout to Montrealers "Vive le Québec libre" did not hesitate to welcome to the Elysée Palace four representatives of the small Acadian community in 1968. These "historic four" were Dr. Léon Richard, then president of the Société Nationale des Acadiens, one of the main organizations for the promotion and development of Acadians in the Maritimes; Adélard Savoie, one of the chief organizers of the 1955 celebrations

MARTINE JACQUOT

Rural France today, in the Poitiers area.

and then president of the young University of Moncton; Gilbert Finn, a future lieutenant-governor of New Brunswick, who was then president of the Acadian financial giant, Insurance Mutual l'Assomption; and Euclide Daigle, at that time vice-president of the Association Acadienne d'Education.

This was not the first contact in modern times between the French and Acadians. In 1859, French historian Edmé Rameau de Saint-Père had published *La France aux colonies: Acadiens et Canadiens*, which allowed Acadians to read about their history in their own language. Rameau de Saint-Père visited the Maritimes in 1860 and corresponded with notable Acadians of his time before publishing a second history of Acadians, *Une colonie féodale en Amérique*, in 1889.

In the 1920s, under the influence of a Comité France-Acadie (France-Acadia Committee) inspired by historian Emile Lauvrière, one of the first to write a history of the Acadians, the French foreign affairs department had sent to Acadie school supplies, books and scholarships. But the 1960s required more, especially in light of the new Quebec-France relationship.

The four Acadians who met with the French president obtained results that form the basis of present-day cooperation: aid for Acadian students, thousands of books for public libraries, a cultural sector for the French consulate which had moved from Halifax to Moncton to better serve the Acadian community, and direct aid for the Acadian daily newspaper at the time, *L'Evangéline*. This was a major breakthrough that helped other enterprises that furthered French-Acadian cooperation, including the private Les Amitiés Acadiennes, founded in 1977, which promotes communication, exchanges and an annual France-Acadie annual award. Acadians were recognized as fellow francophones. France was no longer their country, but was still a powerful relative, able to support smaller communities on the chessboard of international relations.

After de Gaulle, the next French president to come to Acadie was François Mitterand, a major supporter and initiator of the francophone summits, at which Acadians now have their own seats, within the Canadian delegation. In 1987 Mitterand landed briefly in Moncton on the Concorde, the pride of British-French aeronautic cooperation, and visited Caraquet with novelist Antonine Maillet, whom he had named to the Haut Conseil de la Francophonie. During a 1990 stop at Halifax he displayed a precise knowledge of the situation of Nova Scotia's Acadians.

French politicians from all parties have supported French-Acadian links. Current president Jacques Chirac, while he was mayor of Paris, inaugurated in Paris a "Place de l'Acadie," and regional and local contacts are increasingly more numerous. Edith Cresson, the first woman Prime Minister France had (for a brief period in 1991), was well aware when she was Mayor of Châtellerault of the Acadian reality and of its links with France. Father Léger Comeau, a key player in the Société Nationale des Acadiens during the 1970s and 1980s, led several delegations to France to broaden agreements. Direct economic results may not yet be apparent, but international trade fairs based on francophone links are now increasingly common. Investors and business people on both sides of the Atlantic are increasingly attracted by joint ventures, exchanges and other forms of partnership.

New Brunswick, in addition to its participation in international francophone organizations such as the Agence de Coopération Cultur-elle et Technique (Technical and Cultural Cooperation Agency), has a direct bilateral agreement with the Vienne region of France. In a 1984 interview with Acadian writer Melvin Gallant for *Égalité*, an Acadian journal on politics, Jean-Pierre Ouellet, then a minister in the New Brunswick government, stated: "We have obviously always had cultural relations with the area of Poitou, of which Vienne is a part, as most of our ancestors came from there. Now we would like these contacts to develop into economic and social ties for our mutual benefit." The University of Moncton signed a broad agreement with the University of Poitiers, the only French university with an Acadian studies centre at that time. Such contacts benefit the whole com-munity, both in the Maritimes and in France. France of course, is now also one of the main builders of the new Europe and Canadian links with countries in one of the major economic and cultural powers of the next century is an important part of our collective future.

III. Dreams of Riches and Trade Wars

The name of the new land of Acadie comes from one of the first explorers of the Atlantic coast, Giovanni de Verrazzano, a captain from Florence, who had been sent to the New World by François I, King of France, in 1524. Although Verrazzano did not enter the Bay of Fundy, he gave the name Arcadie to a stretch of coastline with particularly beautiful forests. Very quickly the word grew to indicate on maps first the southeastern shore of Nova Scotia (the only part Verrazzano had seen) and finally the whole Nova Scotia peninsula. After 1548, maps carried the word Acadie rather than Arcadie.

Why had the French originally come to Acadie? Major powers act today just like a few centuries ago, primarily for compelling eco-nomic, political and military reasons. Any mission to distant lands costs money and needs to produce some form of profit.

The most obvious reason was economic. In the seventeenth century, people in predominantly Catholic countries such as France were forbidden to eat meat for more than 160 days a year, so demand for fish was high. The most obvious choice was cod, found aplenty on the banks near Newfoundland and Nova Scotia, and in the Gulf of Saint Lawrence. According to Champlain, in 1618 it was possible to fish a million cod annually! Parisians preferred salt cod, known as *morue verte* (which some Acadians call *morue varte*), while the Portuguese and Italians preferred dried cod (sometimes called by Acadians *molue sec*).

Map of Acadie, 1757.

Before Acadie was founded, large numbers of European fishermen and traders had been consorting with North American nations for more than a century. At the beginning of the seventeenth century, France alone sent more than 200 ships to the region. Medium-sized ships with sailors as young as 12 left France in early March to reach the fishing banks and fill up with their load of *morue verte*. Some men fished, some cut the cod and some salted it and piled it in the hull. When full, or as Lent was about to start, the boats sailed back to France, where cod was used in many ways: boiled, in cream sauce, with garlic, or as a stew. Larger ships left later to fish for cod that would be dried; this type of fishing, practised for instance by Nicholas Denys (1598-1688), a famous French merchant and explorer, called for temporary settlements while the fish dried.

The fishing industry was controlled by French companies, and Acadie and New France derived few financial benefits from it. The same was not true, however, of another industry which started in the seventeenth century—the fur trade. Beaver and marten pelts, fox fur, all brought riches to French merchants and the colonies. The felt hats of the day required a large number of beaver hairs, and leather and fur were needed for clothing. At the time of Charles de Saint-Etienne de La Tour (1593-1663) the fur trade was flourishing from the Bay of Fundy to as far as Cape Sable. When Charles de Menou d'Aulnay blocked his trade with France, La Tour traded pelts with New Englan-

Drying cod.

ders—the market was wide open. At Port-Royal and Pentagouet, d'Aulnay and his colonists cultivated the land, but their chief interest was the fur trade. At Cape Sable and Saint John, La Tour's only interest was in trading with Indians for furs. Nicolas Denys, however, primarily sought fish and did less fur and lumber trading. In doing so, he discovered and named places all along the coast of what are today Cape Breton, mainland Nova Scotia and New Brunswick.

The intermingling of economic, private and public interests at that time is exemplified in the conflict between La Tour and d'Aulnay, the Acadian region's "civil war" of the mid-seventeenth century. Men needed to reap profits from the fur trade to pay for ships, materials and loans. La Tour is often accused of having "betrayed" France because he became a baronet under British rule. He had in fact little choice, as this was a way of mortgaging what he owned and reclaiming it. D'Aulnay, officially governor of Acadie, hoped to establish a barony for his heirs and seemed to win in 1645 when he captured Fort La Tour, at the mouth of the Saint John River, while La Tour was in Boston renegotiating for support from New Englanders. D'Aulnay made Madame La Tour a prisoner (and an Acadian heroine) and hanged his rival's soldiers. The lady, who had done all she could to support her husband, died a short time later.

La Tour then went to Quebec City, where civil and religious administrators welcomed him, and resumed his fur trading, even helping Des Groseilliers (one of the most famous coureurs de bois) and others develop trading to the west. When d'Aulnay died in 1650, La Tour sailed to France and returned as governor of Acadie, bringing with him Philip Mius d'Entremont—who founded Pobomcoup (now Pubnico) in 1651 or 1653—as his major general. Money matters, however, were not laid to rest! Emmanuel Le Borgne had lent money to d'Aulnay and wanted to be reimbursed. Jeanne Motin, d'Aulnay's widow, realizing that Le Borgne sought to ruin her, married Charles La Tour in 1653; she was 30, he twice that age. Fighting between the La Tour and Le Borgne interests was stopped abruptly in 1654 by Robert Sedgwick and the New Englanders, who seized forts on the

Arichat-Ouest, Nova Scotia.

Saint John River and at Port Royal and Pentagouet. Sent to England as a prisoner, La Tour resurrected his Scottish title and managed to have his debts paid by two wealthy Englishmen, William Crowne and Thomas Temple. The latter tried to open new trading posts for the British and brought new settlers to Acadie, including the parents of Pierre and Charles Melanson, the ancestors of the Acadian Melansons. La Tour returned to Acadie, where he died in 1663.

Nicholas Denys is one of the most interesting figures of that time. Born in Tours in 1598, he worked for the Company of New France in 1632 and started trading prized white oak wood at La Hève in 1634 but had to go back to France because of financial problems. He came back, trading fish and furs all along the coast of the Gulf of Saint

Lawrence and to Newfoundland. Victimized by d'Aulnay, who confiscated all the goods stocked at Denys' trading post in Miscou, off the Acadian peninsula of New Brunswick, Denys got back his rights from the Company of New France in 1653 and became governor of Acadie, from Canso to Gaspé, in 1654. Author of a major geographic and historic description of New France published in 1672, he well deserves the honour of having an Acadian historical society bear his name today. Several monuments also remind us of his name, from a plaque in Bathurst (Nepisiguit in the eighteenth century) where he died in 1688, to a museum in St. Peters, the Saint-Pierre (or Port-Toulouse) where he established a post in 1650. His brother, Simon Denys, had a trading post at Sainte-Anne (Englishtown), the first European settlement on Isle Royale (now Cape Breton) which served as Port-Dauphin, the capital, from 1713 to 1719.

Private companies had from the start of the Acadian colony been given the task of developing the land. They could invest in ships and trading posts, grant land and sent settlers to North America. Compagnie des Cent-Associés (Company of One Hundred Associates) had been created with that goal in mind when Louis XIII had granted its charter in 1627. In 1663 the charter was revoked and the company disbanded, largely because private economic interests and goals had prevented the placement of enough settlers on the land to counter the New England colonies and offer an agricultural base that could support French armies. Investments were huge. The company had, over thirty-five years, spent 1.2 million French pounds on the Canadian and Acadian colonies. Profits, however, could also be enormous. The French city of Niort in Poitou-Charentes, owed its major glove industry in the eighteenth century to pelts being imported from Canada and Acadie.

IV. Louisbourg

Louisbourg, first called Port Saint-Louis, was founded to supervise and defend the fishing industry and to aid in the recapture of mainland Nova Scotia, which had been given to Britain by the Treaty of Utrecht in 1713. Daniel d'Auger de Subercase, a brilliant officer who had been governor of Acadie from 1706, had valiantly defended Port-Royal but had finally lost it in 1710. Feeling a lack of support from Paris, he refused to be named governor again in 1711. France decided to heavily fortify Port Saint-Louis and it became a large town and a major strategic point. The population of Isle Royale increased from 700 in 1715 to 2,800 by 1723. The fortress, finally completed in 1745, cost millions of French pounds. One popular rumour in France had it that the rooftops of Louisbourg were covered with gold and could be seen from across the Atlantic when the weather was clear.

Louisbourg may not really have been seen from France, but its first lighthouses, built in 1731 and 1736, burned cod oil to guide many a ship to its harbour. The fortress and the colony of Isle Royale were financially successful until the 1730s, largely thanks to the export of fish. Louis-Simon (1674-1738) and Antoine de la Boularderie (1705-71) ran a local trade in fish, coal, lumber and supplies for the huge town and fortress. Not counting local fishing boats, about 154 vessels per year anchored at Louisbourg between 1733 and 1743, making it the fourth largest harbour north of Florida at the time.

Wood and coal were also exported—the French having been the first to operate a coal mine, starting in 1720 at the place now called Port Morien from the French Maurienne. But fish represented 90 per cent of all products exported to France. Merchants at Louisbourg received all kinds of merchandise from various European countries, and they received wood from Canada and sent it to the French Caribbean, along with large quantities of dried cod. In return they received sugar, coffee, molasses and rum, shipping the latter in large quantities to the New England colonies. Sieur de Roma, who had trading posts at Trois-Rivières and on Ile Saint-Jean, had five vessels, and was one of many to follow the trading routes between Canada, Acadie and the Caribbean.

There were few Acadian farmers at Louisbourg. One reason may be that mainland Acadians were forbidden by the British to go there. But also, Acadians were not attracted by the poor soil of Cape Breton and saw no reason to leave their fertile lands, their herds and their homes. The 3,500 inhabitants of Louisbourg were mostly Europeans who stayed only for a few years.

Among the officers in the French army was Thomas Jacau (pronounced Jacko). Born in the Charente maritime region of western France in 1674, he had become master gunner at Port-Royal after moving to America. At Port-Royal in 1705 he had married Anne Melanson, who was to bear him six children. Jacau was highly praised by French officials, particularly by Mathieu de Goutin, then lieutenant-general of the king in Acadie. It is therefore not surprising that he left for Louisbourg in 1710. One of his sons, Louis-Thomas Jacau, born at Louisbourg in 1712, also chose a military career. Known to historians as Jacau de Fiedmont, he became the only Acadian to receive the title of Maréchal (Marshal) after a brilliant career in French armies throughout the world, which included service on Ile Royale, at Quebec and at Fort Beauséjour (now in New Brunswick near the border with Nova Scotia). In 1755 he wrote the famous *Journal du siège de Beauséjour* (Diary of the siege of Fort Beausejour). He died in France after 1792, the darkest period of the first French Revolution known as "la Terreur."

The French lost Louisbourg in 1745 for the first time. They got it back in 1748 but lost it for good ten years later. It was razed to the ground, so much so that any traveller to the region in the 1920s saw

Arrival of Acadians in Louisiana, a painting by Robert Dafford (St. Martinville, Louisiana).

only mounds of rubble where the largest town in the Maritimes in its day had once stood. The Canadian government, conscious of the historic importance of this site for the whole of North America, has invested in the reconstruction of the fortress since the 1960s. Although the whole town may never be rebuilt, we can today picture the importance France gave to it and its Acadian colony.

French travellers and merchants have left us records of those times and the activities that took place. For example, the diaries and letters of Henri Brunet have been preserved. A member of several trading companies, Brunet came to Acadie four or five times between 1672 and 1676. He brought to America salt, flour, fishing gear, needles, hats, shoes, shirts, and many other items, which he sold and traded for fish, oil, tobacco, timber, moose hide and beaver pelts. Brunet had no qualms about trading with merchants in Boston to obtain manufactured goods. He also traded with many Acadian settlers, whose names appear in his ledgers: in 1676 he bought a cow from Jean Pitre at Port-Royal, and he dealt with Pierre Melanson called "LaVerdure," Antoine Babin and Jean Bourg.

French businessmen had fish and furs, traded manufactured goods and made profits. The French kings, however, had not found what they were originally looking for—gold. Acadie was not to be the Eldorado that South America was for Spain and Portugal. Nor did anyone find a passage to the riches of China. Kings became less and less inclined to underwrite the expenses of explorers, merchants or settlers who came to the shores of Acadie, except for military reasons.

V. Decision to Leave France and Voyage to the New World

Why would the ancestors of the Acadians have come to North America? The answer is obvious: to enjoy greater freedom, to have all the land they needed and escape warfare, tax collectors, and the various elites who, until the French Revolution, exploited the peasants of France. Although French artists often idealize the lives of peasants in pre-Revolutionary France, we should not. As Robert Darnton puts it: "The peasants of early modern France inhabited a world of stepmothers and orphans, of inexorable, unending toil, and of brutal emotions... The human condition has changed so much since then that we can hardly imagine the way it appeared to people whose lives were really nasty, brutish and short." Seventeenth-century literature never mentions peasants.

Still, it was no picnic to come to America. Captain Vaudron wrote in 1717: "I have been to Canada seven times, and...I venture to state that the most favourable of those voyages gave me more white hairs than all those I have made elsewhere. It is a continual torment for mind and body."

As M. A. MacDonald describes it when Madame La Tour sailed back from Europe on the *Gillyflower*, "a merchantman of average size (ninety by thirty feet), [she] would endure months of tossing on a ship so small that it could not cleave the waves but rode upon them with a relentless rolling, pitching and tossing motion...The cramped, basically freight-carrying vessels held sickening smells that assailed nostrils and queasy stomachs: the stench of past cargoes of fish or half-cured furs, of unwashed bodies and primitive sanitation... Deaths at sea were common, as dysentery, scurvy, infectious boils and deadly fevers attacked bodies weakened by the monotonous, brine-pickled diet and the insufficient and malodorous water laced with vinegar to make it drinkable."

After a crossing from France, Acadie must have looked like paradise, especially in the summer or early autumn!

It is hardly surprising to find, therefore, names like "Paradis," "Refuge," and other versions of heaven, in place names where l'Acadie was to grow—particularly in its cradle, now the Annapolis Valley of Nova Scotia. There is, however, an additional reason for those names. Originally, many of the French who tried to open settlements on North American soil were of Reformed faith (often hiding it in public) and feeling the intolerance of Catholic kings which grew after the death of Henri IV, were looking for safe havens where their communities could grow. Under the protection of Gaspar Coligny, leader of the Protestant Huguenot faction at the French court during the reign of Charles IX (1560-1574), Jean Ribaud, a captain of Dieppe in Normandy, had founded in 1562 a fledging settlement in South Carolina, called Charlesfort, near a place they had named Port Royal. It lasted a year. In 1564, a second French Huguenot colony, Fort Caroline, under Ribaut's second, René de Laudonnière, with some assistance by the British, faced defeat and destruction at the hands of the Spanish under Menendez, who wanted to keep the region under their control.

Not surprisingly, among the founders of the other Port Royal, in Acadie, four years later, there were several Huguenot gentlemen.

CHAPTER 2

Settlement and Expulsion from the New Land

I. Early Settlement in Acadie

Early European attempts to settle on the Atlantic shores of North America were not successful. After the failures of the Baron de Léry on Sable Island in 1518, and of Ribaud in 1562 and de Laudonière in 1564 to establish Huguenot settlements near the first Port Royal, the Marquis de la Roche brought 50 convicts from the prisons of Normandy to Sable Island in 1598, only to be imprisoned himself the following year. Eleven survivors of his ill-fated group were picked up by French vessels five years later. Attempts at settling other parts of Canada, particularly at Tadoussac in 1600, did not fare much better.

Despite this, the explorer Samuel de Champlain remained convinced that France should establish a settlement on the shores of North America. The regions north of Acadie seemed too cold for settlers to remain all winter, and regions to the south belonged to Spain. The area between Canseau (Canso) and Virginia seemed to offer the best opportunities. Pierre du Gua de Monts (1558-1628) and Champlain carefully prepared their first expedition. Having left Le Havre, France, in March 1604, two vessels reached Sable Island. One, led by French shipowner Dupont-Gravé, set sail again for Canseau and then returned to France loaded with furs obtained by trading with Mi'kmaq first nations.

Meanwhile, Champlain and de Monts explored the coastline to the south. Having reached the Bay of Fundy, they decided to stay on the north shore of St. Croix Island (now Dorchet Island in Maine). The freezing cold of an early winter, lack of food and drink, and scurvy led to the death of half of the 79 courageous settlers, all French except for a few Swiss hired as soldiers by the king of France. De Monts, who had received from King Henry IV of France the official title of vice-admiral of Acadie and the monopoly of trade over a territory from the 40th to the

49th parallel, was so surprised by the fierce North American winter that he nearly brought the survivors back to France.

Instead the French moved to Port Royal, and from there, despite conflicts between France and England that saw the territory change hands over more than a century, grew not only a colony but a people. Little by little, they settled new places along the southern shore of the bay or sailed to other locations along the shores of what is now New Brunswick. This was a time when transportation almost always relied on waterways and maritime routes, not only in France or between Europe and the New World, but also along the shores of the Maritimes and on the many rivers that had to be explored. Acadians were bound, from the start, to rely on the sea.

When de Monts had left Le Havre in 1604, he had with him 120 valiant people, all skilled at their trade—craftsmen, soldiers, carpenters, masons, stone cutters, architects. He also had two Catholic priests and a Protestant minister, for de Monts was himself a nobleman of reformed faith. The reign of Henry IV seemed, after the Edict of Nantes in 1598, to have created a new peaceful and tolerant atmosphere. Of these hired men, those who survived the first winter built the "habitation" at Port-Royal. Little did they know that they were founding not only Acadie but Canada. They had been preceded by Mi'kmaq, with whom the French got along well, by Basque sailors, and by Irish monks and Vikings on Newfoundland's shores.

Difficult times awaited the budding colony. In 1607, de Monts' enemies in France succeeded in having his monopoly revoked. The whole group had to go back to France, even though a number of them, particularly Jean de Biencourt, Sieur de Poutrincourt and eight companions, tried to think of ways of staying. They had fallen in love with the land.

Early setbacks did not, however, mean the end of the Acadian colony. Champlain and de Monts turned their attentions after 1608 to a new colony at Quebec on the St. Lawrence River that promised greater profits for trade and opened better opportunities for urban development, but Poutrincourt came back to Port Royal. His son Biencourt, Claude La Tour and his son Charles, and the first farmer of Acadie, Louis Hébert (who left for Quebec in 1617), came with Poutrincourt and decided to stay.

Louis Hébert is a major founding figure for Canada. He came to Acadie three times between 1604 and 1613, accompanied by his wife Marie Rollet, and one of his daughters might well be the first Acadienne ever born. The little group built a mill, planted crops, tended gardens, and hunted and traded with the Mi'kmaq. The war between England and France raged on, but they stayed, even when New England raider Samuel Argall destroyed their main buildings in 1613. They stayed on even though France seemed to have forgotten its Acadian colony. We can imagine the life of these first French settlers, side by side with their Mi'kmaq friends, who were teaching them new words for tools, birds, plants and foods unknown in Europe that would find their way into Acadian French and look so exotic to French writers of the time.

Poutrincourt invited the lawyer Marc Lescarbot to come to Acadie, where he stayed from May 1606 to the summer of 1607. Everything interested Lescarbot as he travelled through the region—animals, Indians, opportunities he could foresee. When he left for France he had with him the manuscript of his *Histoire de la Nouvelle-France* (History of New France), published in 1609. Contrary to those who saw the new territory as simply a means to fast profits, particularly in the fur trade, he felt that there should be a more sensible way to develop the colony and harvest its resources. His enthusiasm is apparent in the long poem "Les Muses de la Nouvelle-France" (The Muses of New France) which he included in his book. What he could not take with him, however, was the whole set-up of the Théâtre de Neptune (Neptune Theatre), a celebration of Poutrincourt and the ancient god of the sea which took place in the harbour at Port Royal in 1606, with Mi'kmaq and Frenchmen in canoes reciting their lines while Poutrincourt's ship approached.

When Poutrincourt came back with wine, supplies and hope, the settlers decided to have a good time. Marc Lescarbot entertained them, and Champlain organized "L'Ordre du Bon Temps" (Order of Good Cheer) in which everyone took turns in competing to provide the culinary delights served at the daily repast. Each tried his best to outdo the previous contender, which fascinated the Mi'kmaq who were invited to be part of the festivities.

The France Lescarbot found after leaving the shores of Acadie was again torn by civil wars. Following the murder of King Henry IV in 1610, all hell broke loose—Catholic against Protestant, defenders of the king against rival princes. The British, meanwhile, laid claim to Acadie, and Sir William Alexander installed Scottish colonists in the former French possession, renamed Nova Scotia. The destiny of any colony lay in the hands of the major power that led it. When France and England reached an agreement in 1632, the king of England had already asked that the Scottish settlers be sent back to Europe, as Acadie officially belonged again to the French.

The following year, Izaac de Razilly arrived at La Hève, on the south shore of Acadie, with three hundred skilled craftsmen, to establish another settlement in a territory that extended as far south as the Kennebec River in what is now Maine. One of those who came with him was Pierre de Comeau, a young man in his thirties from Burgundy. He moved to Port Royal with Charles de Menou d'Aulnay when Razilly died in 1635, and there married Rose Bayols in 1649. They were, as Léonie Comeau Poirier recalls in *My Acadian Heritage*, "the founders of the Comeau branch of the family in North America." They had nine children, six of them boys. These children were definitely Acadiens.

Champlain's Order of Good Cheer, from a painting by C.W. Jefferys.

One of the first children born in Acadie, André Lasnier, was a Métis, the son of Louis Lasnier from Dieppe and a Mi'kmaq woman. Port-Royal having been abandoned at the time, he was born at Port Latour, in the Cap Sable region. It seemed natural for the French to choose Mi'kmaq companions and wives. Some later settlers, such as the Baron Jean Vincent d'Abbadie de Saint-Castin, whose name survives in the place known in Maine as Castine, carried this attitude not only into private unions but into full-fledged alliances. Arrived in New France in 1655, at age 13, he resided in Pentagouet (now in Maine), married the daughter of an Abenaki chief and, with his Indian allies, threatened New England settlers and British forces around

Boston between 1687 and 1699. Later in the 1750s, Jean-Louis Le Loutre, a French priest who devoted his whole life to Acadians and helped to found the village of Cocagne, was to fight alongside a band of Mi'kmaq to regain the ground lost by French armies. He was one of the many French who learned the Mi'kmaq language to communicate with the first nations of the Maritimes.

HENRI-DOMINIQUE PARATTE

Cocagne, New Brunswick.

In 1650 the whole population of Acadie was about four hundred people and made up of 45 to 50 families of French origin living around Port Royal and La Hève, plus a nomadic group of about 60 men—soldiers, hired hands, and coureurs de bois working in the fur trade for La Tour or Nicholas Denys. Most Acadians can trace their origins to one of those fifty families. Between 1650 and 1713 no additional French families came to the colony. New blood was provided only by the single men who settled among Acadians and married one of their daughters. If we believe Dièreville in his *Voyage à l'Acadie* (1699-1700) and other sources describing Acadie in the seventeenth and eighteenth centuries, Acadian daughters married young, about age 21 as opposed to about 25 in France.

When Acadie passed officially into British hands in 1713, not only did the limited French immigration cease altogether, but a few hundred people (from a total population of about 2,000) went back to France. Had this occurred a few generations before, more might have gone back. By 1713, however, Acadians had settled their lands, their

North American identity was taking root and few left the shores of the Bay of Fundy even though France tried to incite them to go to Ile Saint-Jean (Prince Edward Island) or Ile Royale (Cape Breton). A new society distinct from the French from France was now in place. Most of the younger generations had never known France. Their only country was Acadie.

Many Acadians had the same last names and so early on techniques were used to distinguish people with the same first and last names. For instance to distinguish two Pierre Comeaus, one was called "des Loups Marins" (Sealhunter) and the other "L'Esturgeon" (Sturgeon). After a few generations, such nicknames became even more necessary. Acadians also resorted to using "à" to list ancestors after an individual's first name, most last names being similar, as in "Pierrot à Pierrot à Pierre, une descendance du premier Cormier à s'en venir des vieux pays" (Little Peter, son of Little Peter, son of Peter, son of the first Cormier to have come from the old country), a character in *L'Acadie pour Quasiment Rien* (A Free Ride in Acadie) by Antonine Maillet. It may have been a useful tool to distinguish people before 1755. After the Expulsion, it became an essential tool to keep alive the memory of family history and traditions, and many an Acadian child would learn his place in the world by reciting his or her genealogy. Nicknames sometimes served as place names: Aux Loups-marins is one of the places on the Dauphin (Annapolis) River at Port Royal, where many other poetic names could be found, such as A Vallée de misère, A la Renaudière and Au Vert Pré.

The French colony of Acadie of the seventeenth and eighteenth centuries was a peaceful haven as well as a chessboard for competing trade interests and rival empires. The two intermingled easily. Acadian farmers enjoyed a degree of freedom unheard of in Europe at the time. The farms of the Comeau brothers and their Acadian friends were large, their herds well-fed, their lands rich. Little by little, farmers moved along the bay to Les Mines (Minas, Nova Scotia), or Chipoudie (Shepody, New Brunswick) as Albert Thibaudeau and his sons did in 1699, or to Chignectou as did Jacques Bourgeois in 1672.

Acadian farmers gradually moved away from the conflicts that plagued Port Royal, sometimes between the French and the English, sometimes between the French themselves. Port Royal, which had been moved upstream from the original habitation by d'Aulnay in 1636, fell at regular intervals into British hands: from 1654 to 1667, from 1690 to 1692 and finally in 1710, when the area of Port Royal became Annapolis Royal, named for a British queen.

Acadie as a French colony officially ceased to exist in 1713, although France kept territories in the region until the 1750s (present-day New Brunswick, Cape Breton and Prince Edward Island) and tried repeatedly during the first half of the eighteenth century, at a time when its armies were dominant over Europe, to regain control of the region. By then, however, Acadians had begun to identify themselves as a separate people. Along with their Indian friends, they were the only permanent settlers of the huge territory now known as the Maritimes. They were no longer "French from France." They had their own political and social organization, their own imaginative ways of cultivating land along the Bay of Fundy, and they had become a fairly affluent group compared to average French peasants. They had grown used to freedom and space. They had learned to trade

"Settlement of Old Acadie," by Nelson Surette.

with New England without bothering too much about who might officially be in control of Acadie. Some of them had become very powerful business people.

The Acadians' New England neighbours had often come to the New World seeking a life in accordance with their religious or individual wishes, and then, quickly built towns and cities and developed industry as well as agriculture. The French people who came to Acadie came with the blessing of the French government, but the number of settlers was never very high. About 440 Acadians were present in 1651, 1,436 in 1701, and about 10,500 in 1748, while the

50,000 people who inhabited New England in 1641 had grown to about 1.5 million in 1754. Even New France (Quebec today) was no match in size for New England. It had no more than 85,000 inhabitants in 1754.

Acadian culture was not an urban culture. Most Acadians' ancestors had been farmers in France and most were farmers too. When Pierre Thibodeau, born in Poitou in 1631, arrived in Acadie with LeBorgne in 1654, he quickly named the lands granted to him *Prée Ronde* (now Round Hill) and built a grist mill on the river. Port Royal, with about 1,750 inhabitants in 1750, could not be compared with Quebec City. The region known as Les Mines (around Grand Pré today) was then by far the largest settlement, with 5,000 Acadians, the region of Beaubassin (communities around Chignecto Bay, the former Chignectou) having grown to be second in importance with 2,800. Acadians made up a distinct North American community, largely ready to assume control of its own affairs. The early eighteenth century, unfortunately, was a little too early for such an attitude to be understood, especially when the claim was made by "lowly" peasants at a time when France or England were still dominated by aristocracies. When Acadians, through their community elders, tried to be recognized by England as "French neutrals," their claims were rejected. They were scattered all over the world and their Acadie was taken from them, their homes destroyed, their possessions plundered, their families divided.

II. An Original Culture

> In each Acadian there is a nostalgic dream of quiet paths
> through endless forests, of the soft pounding of waves calling
> to adventures at sea…All Acadians are primarily country folk,
> whose wish it is to live in peace, in their own parishes,
> between the forest and the sea. Could they, however, live now
> as they did in the past?
>
> -Jean-Claude Vernex, *Les Acadiens*

Acadians were the first group of European origin to adjust to North America and modify its landscape. They organized their lives in a way that harmonized with the Maritime environment. The experiences of the sauniers (workers in saltworks) with the salt marshes of Saintonge and Aunis in France and the experiences of farmers from Poitou who had learnt from the Dutch how to drain marshlands by building dykes proved valuable in the New World. Settlers in New

France cleared the land near the St. Lawrence River, cutting trees and clearing stones, but Acadians found, starting along the Dauphin River at Port Royal, that a system of dykes, levees and *aboiteaux* (long wooden boxes at the base of the dykes with a valve that allowed water to flow out to the sea but not inland) enabled them to reclaim much richer lands, around the rivers and the Bay of Fundy, than they could have had by clearing the uplands.

In his book *Voyage à l'Acadie* (1708), Dièreville, who had come to Port Royal as the representative of a fishing company, marvelled at the way Acadians built their dykes. "They plant five or six rows of huge whole trees at those locations where the sea enters the marshes, and between each row they lay other long trees on top of one another. Then they fill the cracks with thick clay, so that no water can go through any longer. In the midst of this levee they install a wooden clapper valve (an esseau) that, at low tide, lets the water drain from the marshes, while preventing salt water from the sea to flow into the marshlands. Such work is hard and takes many days... but, when it is done, when after the first year soft water from the rains has washed away most of the salt from the new lands, they reap all they need to obtain from it."

Dièreville could not praise enough the skills shown by Acadians in farming their lands, in producing the wheat, flax, vegetables and fruit they needed, in feeding their cattle, sheep and horses. He noticed how it had been necessary for them to create a communal system, the work needed to build the dykes being far too much for any individual farmer.

In a song, modern Acadian singer Calixte Duguay recalls with nostalgia those *aboiteaux*, trademarks of the rich lands of the old Acadie that were taken from Acadians. The only region where that old Acadie of the marshlands remained in Acadian hands was along the Memramcook River, whose valley, one of the important agricultural centres in New Brunswick, was a major reconstruction centre for the new Acadie after the Expulsion.

On those lands Acadians not only grew wheat and raised cattle, but also grew barley, rye, and peas in quantities abundant enough for selling and trading. They grew flax and hemp to make their own clothes, and used the wool from their sheep. Fruit grew in large quantities, and Governor Villebon in 1699 declared that "Port Royal, as far as apples go, is as rich as a little Normandy." One could still see Acadian apple trees in the Annapolis Valley in the 1930s. One could also find pears and cherries. Acadians at Les Mines grew grapes, a tradition that was picked up again by Grand Pré wines only in the 1980s, with wines such as "L'Acadie Blanc" or "L'Acadie Rouge," or by the winery at Falmouth, formerly Sainte-Famille de Pisiquid.

Although they brought with them traits common to the rural cultures of the regions they came from, Acadians had created by the 1740s their own brand of culture, with distinct regions, a strong business community and a very open attitude to all of North America. The romantic story of Evangeline, whose Yankee author had little direct knowledge of Acadians, relied on former French writings describing l'Acadie as a rural paradise. How real was that idyllic image?

A modern painting by Nelson Surette depicts Acadian farmers piling hay on stacks, with Cap Baptiste (Cape Blomidon) in the background. Women wore wooden clogs with wool socks, a long striped wool skirt, and a white shirt under a black bodice laced in front. A scarf, knotted in front, covered their shoulders and they wore a simple white hat. Sometimes, to work at home, women wore an apron. For men, ordinary clothes were also simple: clogs, wool socks, short trousers, a shirt similar to those of the women, maybe a vest, and sometimes a felt hat. They might dress better sometimes, wearing leather shoes with a buckle, instead of clogs, and a vest and jacket. In the wintertime, an Acadian may have done what a man in Louisbourg did to keep his feet warm: stuff his or her clogs with straw. Some adopted Indian moccasins. They had plenty of wool—cleaned, carded, spun and woven at home—and had little problem obtaining durable warm clothes.

Although the climate of the Maritimes was not much different from the climate of western France in the summertime, it was definitely colder during the long winters. But Acadian pioneers do not seem to have suffered excessively. They had plenty of wood and supplemented the food they grew with what they hunted, fished, trapped or traded. Their Indian friends showed them many things. They became quite proficient at curing fish, young people often working for fishing companies.

Wintertime was, as in many rural societies until the end of the nineteenth century, a time to catch up on what summer had not left time to do. Men used wood to make furniture for the house—tables, chairs, beds, cradles, sideboards and benches—and farm implements, from hoes and flails to cartwheels. Women spun the wool and wove cloth, attending to all household needs. Families being large, they probably had little time to themselves. In Acadian villages, with clean air and healthy food, children grew up strong, and infant mortality was noticeably lower than in Europe at the time. Acadian society was, by and large, an affluent society.

Wood was the basic material used to construct houses. Acadians built their own homes, usually assisted by family and friends, and must have been quite skilled at it, despite the fact that a 1671 census lists only two carpenters and one mason. Houses were fairly large. Four houses at Port Royal and a house in Bellisle measured about 32 by 25 feet. They were low, however, usually of one floor, sometimes a floor and a half. If there was a loft (a *gornier*, as there usually was in most Acadian houses in later centuries), it was probably left unused, being frightfully cold because of the lack of insulation under the roof.

Many Acadian houses consisted of a wooden frame of rough timber on a foundation of dry masonry, giving the building a rectangular shape, with a few windows and a door. Once the frame was in place, held together by wooden pegs, the cracks were filled with straw and mud, and the whole surface was covered with clapboard or plaster. To preserve the house from cold in winter, windows had

HENRI-DOMINIQUE PARATTE

Forge Lenoir, Ile Madame, Nova Scotia.

shutters. Roofs were made of thatch (as discovered at Bellisle), boards, or shingles of cedar or birchbark (the wood that made Indian canoes watertight). Every house probably had a fireplace made of clay on sticks, and some had ovens.

The family remained a strong unit among Acadians. Community elders were elected to rule over the affairs of the villages and communicate with colonial authorities. Although parish priests were often among the few people who knew how to read and write, a lay elite was increasingly present and Acadians proved fiercely independent minded. Acadians lived in peace, and traded with New England merchants as well as with the French or the West Indies. They cared little, on the whole, for which "official" political regime they lived under, though they obviously felt closer to France than to British military administrators, for whom they were not only North American, but Catholic and French.

If life for the Acadians was not paradise, not quite a garden of Eden, it was nevertheless a prosperous one in a country they liked. Everything, from the size of their cattle to the size of their families, confirms their overall well-being. A man like Nicolas Gautier, born in Rochefort in 1689, married to Marie Allain, was in 1744 owner of flour mills, saw mills, herds of cattle, trading with Boston and the Antilles: a fortune of 80,000 livres that would be stolen during the Expulsion. It would be years before his descendants would resettle in St. Pierre and Miquelon. No wonder tales of hidden treasures are still very much alive, all around the old Acadian lands on the shores of Fundy.

The Expulsion not only destroyed lives, it ruined a whole society. The names of the deported can be found today in the Acadian regions which they settled after their return. The Allards are found in Allardville in northern New Brunswick, the Arsenaults on Prince Edward Island, the Aucoins in Chéticamp, the Babineaus and the Bastaraches in southeastern New Brunswick, the Beaulieus in Madawaska, the Belliveaus in L'Anse-desBelliveau in southwestern Nova Scotia, and the Blanchards at Caraquet. There are the Bourques, Boudreaus, and Chiassons; the Comeaus so numerous at Baie Sainte Marie; the Cormiers and the Daigles. The d'Entremonts founded West Pubnico. The Dugas were the first to reach Baie Sainte-Marie. Forests, Gallants, Gaudets, Girouards, Godins, Hachés, Henrys, Landrys, LeBlancs, Légers, Maillets, Melansons, Pîtres, Poiriers, Pothiers, Robichauds, Roys, Samsons, Saulniers, Surettes, Thériots, Thibodeaus are many other typical Acadian family names. The names are recognizable even though some were changed later to avoid being attacked because of ethnic prejudice—Amirault becoming Amiro, Daigle becoming Eagles, Leblanc changed to White, Brun to Brine.

Acadians were founders not only of Canada, but of a whole new world. Even though the first attempts at settling Ile Saint-Jean in 1720 had failed, some Acadian families had stayed. Michel Haché-Gallant (born in Acadie in 1660) and Anne Cormier were the core of the first white family established at Port-Lajoie (now Charlottetown) in 1720, and they had many children. Any person named Gallant in Canada or in the United States is probably related to them. A monument at the Port La Joye/Fort Amherst historic park was erected to their memory in 1965 by their descendants. Much of the same could be said of all Acadian families, and "Les Retrouvailles" in New Brunswick in 1994 was the major part of the Congrès Mondial Acadien, and proved that some families had hundreds of thousands of descendants all over the world, like the LeBlancs or the Girouards.

When Antonine Maillet wrote her comic sketch "Les bancs d'église" (church pews) in her play *La Sagouine*, she made fun of the oldest families, the ones who had had pews since their return from deportation and did not want to relinquish their status and power by accepting that the poor could lease their pews for the coming year. In the eyes of many, until recently, no one whose ancestors were not there before 1755 could claim to be a "true" Acadian. This vision is limited: no community can grow without immigrants, and there were even in the old Acadie people of Basque and Irish origin. Yet nothing can change the fact that the old Acadie is the homeland that defined Acadians. It is still present in the names and in the memories. From 1755 on, Acadie would be forever in the hearts and minds of Acadians, whatever changes the societies that they lived in went through.

III. Pawns in the Hands of Major Powers

> Thus it is peremptorily his Majesty's orders, that the whole French inhabitants of these districts be removed; and I am, through His Majesty's goodness, directed to allow you liberty to carry off your money and household goods, as many as you can without discommoding the vessels you go in.
> -Colonel John Winslow, Grand-Pré,
> September 2, 1755

Acadians were deported in 1755 because some British officers felt they might turn against them, because it seemed safer to have Protestant settlers on their lands, and because their lands and estates were among the richest on the Atlantic seaboard.

Caught between the two largest colonial powers in the world, Acadians were used to being governed alternately by the French and the British, to changes at Port Royal and raids by privateers from New England. They paid a price every time a fight broke out between New France and New England. In 1690 when France had attacked the New England colonies under Pierre Le Moyne d'Iberville, one of the founders of Louisbourg, Acadians had seen their dykes destroyed in retaliation. On the whole, however, they withstood well the many dangers their little group had to fear. They felt they belonged to Acadie, not to France or England, and that their neutrality should be recognized. They were Republicans in North America before the United States.

When in 1744, at the height of the golden age of the old Acadie, Captain De Gannes, one of the French officers trying to convince Acadians that France was about to regain control of the colony, talked to Acadians from Les Mines (Grand Pré), Rivière aux Canards (Canard River) and "Péjéguit" (Windsor), the elders of the community pleaded with him to withdraw troops from their lands, and insisted that they had little to contribute to help French soldiers. However, a few rich Acadians decided to help the same military expedition, led

RENÉ BELIVEAU

"Oath of Allegiance, 1730" by Nelson Surette.

by Francois du Pont Duvivier. Joseph LeBlanc, called "Le Maigre" (Skinny One, 1697-1772), and Nicolas Gaultier, called "Bellair" (Nice Looking One, 1689-1752), for commercial and personal reasons convinced some of their friends. Yet the majority of Acadians were more cautious, knowing full well that even a victorious military operation in North America did not mean that France would win its old colony back.

As it turned out, neither the expeditions of Duvivier and his

French-Indian force in 1744, and similar ones in 1745 and 1746, nor the ill-fated French fleet under the Duc d'Anville sent in 1746 to recapture Louisbourg, Nova Scotia and New France were able to change the balance of power.

Acadians were cautious, but they nevertheless resisted their British rulers. They found reasons not to pay taxes, not to work on forced labour projects and not to take oaths of allegiance that would have broken their vows to remain neutral. They rejected all attempts made by French allies of the English to tie them to British interests. Thomas Pichon, a former assistant to Governor Raymond at Louisbourg in 1751 turned spy for England, tried hard but without success to get them to turn against France. Although a number moved to Beaubassin or Ile Saint-Jean in the years before the Expulsion, Acadians remained strong in their declared determination not to be involved in a conflict in which they felt both sides were trying to use them to their advantage.

For a long time British administrators seemed to accept the fact that Acadians were entitled to stay on their lands. Although leery, British authorities still needed the Acadians to supply their soldiers with food, wood and labour. They did not grant them much say, however, in the way the colony should be ruled. Acadian representatives were there only to express the desires of the population and to carry orders from the colonial authorities. The British repeatedly insisted on the need for the Acadian population to swear an unqualified oath of allegiance. Governor Richard Phillips accepted an oath of neutrality from the Acadians in 1729-30, but higher authorities were apparently not informed: this was a time of high incompetence and inefficiency in the whole British political system, and politically astute decisions usually came second to military expediency.

The situation until 1749 was a strange one in many ways. British officers wanted to develop a colony that corresponded to their own wishes, but somehow the large number of British settlers expected did not materialize. Acadians were not supposed to farm new land but did so anyway and spread into new areas such as Memramcook River, Petitcodiac and Chipoudie. The treaty of Utrecht guaranteed the right of Catholics to their faith, but the laws of Britain did not allow it. In this administrative limbo the Catholic clergy retained their importance in Acadian life. Acadians would be deported for supposedly strategic reasons—yet England and France were not at war at the time of the Expulsion.

The demand upon Acadians in 1749 to take an unqualified oath of allegiance to the British Crown caused many to seek refuge on Ile

Saint-Jean and Ile Royale. Their numbers grew quickly on Ile Saint-Jean, from 250 to 1,720 to 5,000 in 1755. They fought extreme hardships to clear the land, to build homes, mills and churches and to produce enough food for themselves and the French garrison at Louisbourg. Meanwhile France, to defend its disputed boundaries and match British forts, constructed Fort Beauséjour in 1751. Jean-Louis Le Loutre actively tried to get Acadians and Indians to support French interests. On the English side, Charles Lawrence, named Governor of Nova Scotia in 1753, and Governor Shirley of Massachusetts decided to dislodge the French from the Chignecto area. Lieutenant-Colonel Monckton captured Fort Beauséjour in June 1755 and this victory opened the way to two tragic forerunners of the Expulsion of the Acadians. First, it was decided to expel Acadians from the region so that settlers loyal to England could prevent any attempt by the French to use the area as a base for raids against mainland Nova Scotia. Second, the presence of Acadians inside Fort Beauséjour, although they claimed to have been there as captives, offered a good pretext for the British to claim that Acadians were disloyal, and wage war openly against them.

Were they disloyal? It all depends on how things are viewed. Historians of Loyalist stock have generally taken the view that Acadians were disloyal as long as their attitudes helped the French. We know that, in 1744, Acadians at Les Mines clearly told some French soldiers that they did not want to be officially involved. But how could they have avoided some degree of involvement, with the British indicating more and more clearly that they had no intention of letting Acadians live their lives in peace on their own lands?

France at the time had the upper hand on most fronts, even though Louis XV wanted peace first and foremost. As French historian Michel Antoine recalls in his biography of Louis XV, in 1755 General Braddock and his lieutenants had suffered a severe defeat while attempting to attack French forts. "Their attempt was a disaster, and Braddock was fatally wounded... The huge British campaign in North America had led to the capture of two vessels only, and the total failure of all land attacks. New England governors and the London government were sorely disappointed." Acadians knew how things were going. Unfortunately, they were the weak part of the French empire, and history shows us that mighty empires have little pity for the weak. The Expulsion of the Acadians may be seen as an attempt by the British to prove that victory might in the long run be possible. How could Acadians, being of French origin, not have rejoiced privately at British defeats and French victories?

"The Embarkation" by Nelson Surette.

French and Acadian historians now view the fact that some Acadians took part in battles alongside the French against the English not as a proof of their disloyalty to anyone—confusion at the time being extreme—but as a proof that Acadians, far from being a flock of sheep ready to be slaughtered, unequivocally asserted their identity as a people by standing up and fighting. A study by French historian Robert Sauvageau, *Acadie: la guerre de cent ans des Français d'Amérique* (Acadie: the hundred-year war of the French in America), has brought to light many events that had been until now untold or overlooked. For example, there were Acadian privateers in the eighteenth century. There were many proud military events throughout Acadian history, from the thirty-year war led by the Baron de Saint-Castin, to the attack on Annapolis Royal led in 1711 by the priest Antoine Gaulin. Acadians were among the defenders of Fort Beauséjour, and among the defenders of Quebec City in 1759. Acadians were present when French guns were last heard on the Restigouche River on July 8, 1760. They had moved a year earlier to the area, where French Capuchin missionaries had worked with Indians since 1745 (one of them, Père Pacifique, having produced a dictionary and the Gospels in the Mi'kmaq language).

However, one should be careful not to think that Acadians were necessarily involved in all guerrilla warfare operations against the

Acadian hooked rug depicting the Expulsion.

British. French agents, such as Jean-Louis Le Loutre, were often operating against the British with Mi'kmaq Indians, and sometimes Mi'kmaq Indians operated on their own, for example, when they burned Beaubassin in 1750.

According to Sauvageau, several incompetent French officers tried, wrongly, to blame Acadians for their own failures. This was the case of Vergor, in charge of the defence of Fort Beauséjour. Several trials called the "Canadian trials" took place in France after 1763. Among the accused was Charles de Boishébert, who left a long document about the heroic resistance of Acadians and Canadians throughout the Seven Years' War. Major mistakes were made by governors of New France who forgot that, as Frontenac had said, Acadie was "the main pillar of the French fortress in North America." Other mistakes were made by Parisian administrators not daring enough, and by officers not brilliant enough and in a hurry to go back to France. Acadian militias were not used by the French as much as they could have been against British authorities, who considered Acadians to be prisoners of war even in peacetime, against all rules.

It is important, to view Acadians as an intelligent and well-organized community and not as passive peasants waiting to be expelled. They were not cowards, nor were they traitors. They were deported while England and France were not officially at war—one of the reasons Louisiana lawyer Warren Perrin petitions the Queen of

French Cross at Morden, Nova Scotia.

England today is to definitely rescind Expulsion orders. During hard times over which they had little control, they defended what they felt they should defend, sometimes with caution like a fox, sometimes openly like Beausoleil Broussard or those unknown Acadians who defeated British soldiers in war at Bridgetown in 1757, in the famed "Battle of Bloody Creek."

Beausoleil Broussard, whose name was adopted by an Acadian folk-rock group of the 1980s and who appears in Alphonse Deveau's historical novel *Le chef des Acadiens* (1956), in Antonine Maillet's *Pélagie-la-Charrette* (1979) and in Claude LeBouthillier's novel *Le Feu du Mauvais Temps* (1989), is a mesmerizing figure in Acadian history. Born Joseph Broussard at Port Royal in 1702, he went to reside at Le Cran (south of Moncton) in 1740 and took part in raids against the English in 1747. Declared an outlaw that same year, he was involved in raids again in 1755 when French and English forces fought around Beauséjour. He kept fighting in the woods, with a small band of Acadians, until his surrender in 1758. Freed from British jails in 1763, he went to Louisiana where his family lived. His nickname, "Beausoleil," (Bright Sun) is a clear indication that he was one of the heroes in Acadian history who stood his ground, fighting valiantly until all hope was lost. Were Broussard alive today he would probably be called a "freedom fighter." So would many other Acadians. The Beausoleil family in Louisiana is extremely proud of its ancestor.

In July 1755, Governor Lawrence ordered Acadian deputies to appear before him in Halifax to take an unqualified oath of allegiance to the Crown of England. They refused and were thrown into prison and eventually deported. That same year, between October and the end of January, 7,000 Acadians were deported from Nova Scotia. Several ran away, hid in the woods, fled to Québec or Ile Saint-Jean, or tried to remain in remote corners of the province. Some attacked British troops, without much hope of swaying the balance of power. Those who fled were chased by soldiers, taken prisoner or shot. Some were kept, as on the DesBarres estate, as unpaid labourers to mend the dykes they had built to protect their own lands. The cruel irony was even more striking when we think that Joseph-Frédéric Wallet DesBarres himself (who was among other functions, lieutenant-governor of Cape Breton from 1784 to 1787) was of French Huguenot origin, but also an officer in the armies of Britain, somewhat like Swiss-French officer Sir George Prevost, who was named lieutenant-governor of Nova Scotia in 1808.

In some areas, such as Cape Sable, Acadians were deported only later. For Acadians who surrendered or were taken prisoner the process ended in 1764. The larger group was rounded up and deported by New England and British soldiers in 1755.

These early deportees, depicted in visual representations of the Expulsion such as Nelson Surette's paintings or the paintings by Claude Picard now in the memorial church at Grand Pré, were from Les Mines, Pisiquid, Port Royal and Chignectou. At Les Mines, all males over the age of 10 were kept prisoners in the church of Saint-Charles; at Pisiguid and Chignectou they were kept in forts; and at Port Royal, Acadians were kept in their homes until December, when they were deported. They could take no more than they could carry, so in a matter of a few days they were transformed from independent landowners to destitute exiles. Different types of boats then transported them to Massachusetts, Connecticut, Pennsylvania, New York, Maryland, North Carolina, South Carolina, Georgia and Virginia.

Virginia refused to accept Acadian deportees, and those who were to go there were sent back to England where they were kept until 1763, when a number were allowed to go to France or make their way to the New World again. The American colonies were not ready for them and were not pleased with French people with few resources being thrown into the midst of their populations. Being Catholics made them even more unpleasant in the view of those New Englanders, who were particularly opposed to "popery." These were times of intense religious fanaticism. Acadians had little to do with it, and yet they found themselves in the midst of another conflict.

Most Acadians were ill-treated nearly everywhere they were sent. One group kept as prisoners at Halifax was employed to fortify the town against potential French assailants, while others were sent to Great Britain as prisoners. Many died in the wet and cold prisons, neglected and malnourished. At Bristol, for example, 184 of 300 prisoners died. In his essay *The Acadian Exiles in Pennsylvania*, William B. Reed states that "It was certainly an unpropitious time for French Roman Catholics to come to those Puritan or Protestant colonies... It was the time when an Indian and a Frenchman were looked on with equal horror."

Acadian exiles faced starvation and were forced to beg and ask for charity; some of their requests were rejected by British authorities because they were in French, and many died. Was this what Lawrence had intended? Anyone with even a minimal understanding of international politics must have known that sending Acadians to the New England colonies was a way to get rid of them, not a resettlement. It may be that, in the view of British officers at the time, 7,000 peasants did not weigh much in the balance of the whole war.

Acadians, for whatever reason, had been pawns in the hands of the major powers. It is no wonder that most of those who survived decided to move back to the Maritimes or to join their fellow French Catholics in Canada, be it on foot, in carts driven by oxen, or by boat. Few remained in the United States even though some would make their way down to Louisiana. Basile Lanoue, born near Port Royal, did

The statue of Evangeline at Grand-Pré.

Cross at Grand-Pré, left. Right: Jolene Adam, director of the Acadian memorial in St. Martinville, Louisiana, in front of the flame.

become a representative in North Carolina in 1796, and Joseph Cyr was elected a Maine representative in 1844, and three Acadians were elected to the first Lousiana legislature in 1805. But these are isolated cases, although many would later (like members of the Mouton family in Louisiana) reach positions of importance in the U.S.

Although the first concern of Acadians was obviously to survive during this troubled period, some have left behind written and oral testimony of the massacres and the deportation. Oral records were passed on in families, and it is in part from this oral tradition that novelist Antonine Maillet was able to write *Pélagie-la-Charrette*, a story of return to the Maritimes from New England. Oral testimony given by Cécile Murat to her granddaughter Sister Marie-Bernard enabled Alphonse Deveau to reconstruct Murat's diaries, published in 1963. In *le Journal de* (The Diary of) *Cécile Murat* we learn how Casimir LeBlanc, uprooted from his Pisiguid home, was shipped to Liverpool, England, and then to Saint-Malo, France, before coming back to Baie Sainte-Marie. The letters of Vénérande Robichaux, born at Port Royal in 1753, reveal how, following the deportation, she spent twenty years in Boston with her family before settling in

The Acadian house and garden reconstructed in Annapolis Royal (Historical Gardens), Nova Scotia. Right: Evangeline's Oak, St. Martinville, Louisiana.

Quebec. From there she wrote continually to members of her family in the Miramichi region of New Brunswick before her death in 1839. Her letters are among the important Acadian documents from the nineteenth century and were published in part in 1887. Not only did she write to preserve the sense of community in her own family circle, but she also described the social, political and religious events of her time with great understanding. More new documents are surfacing all the time.

Surprisingly, some French-speaking settlers were on the side of the British at the time. As early as 1748, British authorities had tried to encourage European Protestants to emigrate to Nova Scotia. Besides French Huguenots who had left France a century earlier, the only other French-speaking European Protestants were people from certain areas of Switzerland. Gédéon Delesderniers, a Vaudois of Huguenot origin, came with his family to Halifax in 1749 where he met his nephew, Moise Delesderniers, who was trying with another Swiss from Neuchâtel, Abraham Dupasquier, to bring over more Swiss immigrants. Three hundred came to Halifax and then moved on to Lunenburg between 1749 and 1757—among them francophones such as Pierre Delaroche, a Protestant minister from Geneva, Jacques Laurent and Jean-Pierre Marguerat, both reserve lieutenants. Isaac Deschamps (1722-85) came to Halifax in 1749 and was called upon to serve as a magistrate before becoming chief justice of Nova Scotia in 1785. Some of these Swiss were involved in discussions with Acadian leaders, but they were not on the side of Acadians. In 1755 official allegiance to the British Crown, religious beliefs and personal interests weighed more heavily than common language. It took a long time before "Swiss" in popular French-Canadian speech stopped carrying the meaning of "Protestant" and "traitor."

The Acadians—hunted like animals, stripped of most of their possessions—might have been totally wiped out in the storm that historians call either "the Expulsion" or "the Deportation" and which Acadian themselves have called le Grand Dérange-ment (the Great Tragic Times). That event gave Providence author Katherine Reid Williams a basis for her rich 1841 novel *The Neutral French* about Acadians, and, five years later, Boston romantic poet H. W. Longfellow his famous poem *Evangeline* (1847), which trans-lated into French by Pamphile Le May, provided Acadians and others with a tragic heroine to use as a symbol of their destiny. No less than four Hollywood movies were made about Evangeline, in 1908, 1911, 1919 and 1929! Most Acadian villages today have a festival with the selection of Evangeline and her fiancé Gabriel as Acadians of the year. A statue of Evangeline faces the rebuilt museum/church in the historic park at Grand Pré, and another statue of Evangéline Bellefontaine can be found in Louisiana. She may never have existed, but she personified the tragic destruction of the world the Acadians had built as their own during the seventeenth and the eighteenth centuries. As Acadian poet Herménégilde Chiasson wrote, "First there was the land and then only a giant grave above which the murmur of distress and wandering could be heard."

CHAPTER 3

Later History in the Maritimes

I. Starting Again

Acadians who came back to the Maritimes, came out of the woods or were released from prison camps faced a depressing and seemingly impossible situation. Their lands had been taken by New England Planters, Loyalists or other Protestant settlers, their rights were of small concern to authorities and they had little material wealth. Their history from then on until at least the 1960s is therefore one of "catching up," in an environment that usually granted them as little as it could.

Primarily farmers before the Expulsion, most Acadians had to become fishermen afterwards in order to survive. And most were no longer their own masters but moved into a seemingly endless cycle of work and debt, as fisheries around the Gulf of Saint Lawrence, from Chéticamp to Gaspé, were controlled throughout the nineteenth century by others, particularly *les Jersiais*, traders from the island of Jersey who had, as British citizens, a monopoly on credit and the labour market. As early as 1763, Jacques Robin, a French Protestant from Jersey, convinced Acadians to go to the Miramichi area to work for him as fishermen in the Gulf of Saint Lawrence. In 1764, the Board of Trade in London authorized Acadians to come back in small groups, provided they would take an oath of allegiance to the king of England. Acadians now had little choice—the Maritimes were firmly under British control.

For most, the sea became their life. It became the way to the outside world and to knowledge of events beyond the borders of the small villages in which Acadians tried to protect their way of life. The sea became the way to earn a living and it gave Acadian villages a most characteristic layout, with a wharf in the middle where people would gather and talk, and where women would wait for men coming

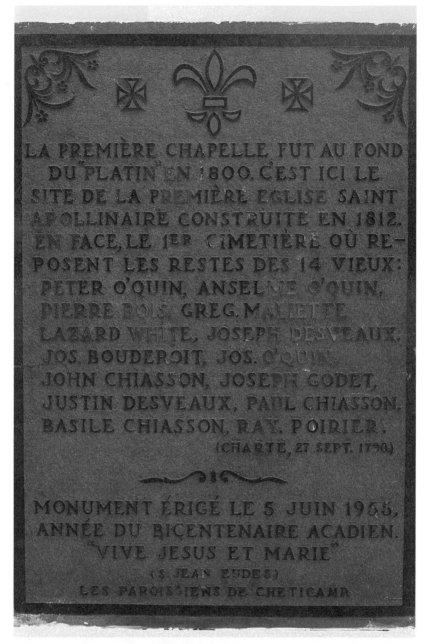

LA PREMIÈRE CHAPELLE FUT AU FOND
DU PLATIN EN 1800. C'EST ICI LE
SITE DE LA PREMIÈRE ÉGLISE SAINT
APOLLINAIRE CONSTRUITE EN 1812.
EN FACE, LE 1ᵉᴿ CIMETIÈRE OÙ RE-
POSENT LES RESTES DES 14 VIEUX:
PETER O'QUIN, ANSELME O'QUIN,
PIERRE BOIS. GREG. MALLETTE
LAZARD WHITE, JOSEPH DESVEAUX,
JOS. BOUDROIT, JOS. O'QUIN,
JOHN CHIASSON, JOSEPH GODET,
JUSTIN DESVEAUX, PAUL CHIASSON,
BASILE CHIASSON, RAY. POIRIER.
(CHARTE, 27 SEPT. 1790)

MONUMENT ÉRIGÉ LE 5 JUIN 1955,
ANNÉE DU BICENTENAIRE ACADIEN.
"VIVE JESUS ET MARIE"
(S. JEAN EUDES)
LES PAROISSIENS DE CHÉTICAMP

Monument to the elders, Chéticamp.

back. Unfortunately, their men did not always come back, making the sea both a source of life and a source of tragedy.

Acadian regions took on a unique appearance: rows of small houses, usually white but sometimes painted with bright colours, long roads close to the shore with a church spire in the middle. Acadians tried to balance their new way of life with the ancient, working at sea, working in the woods, working in old dykelands when they could, as in the Memramcouque (Memramcook) valley. The sea became part of the Acadian imagination and was used for trading, smuggling, bootlegging and carrying on a way of life.

Acadian women must have been as strong as their men. They gave birth to large families, and the Acadian population grew faster than the anglophone, especially in New Brunswick. In 1803, Monsignor Denaut, Bishop of Quebec, estimated that there were only about 8,600 Acadians. In Nova Scotia there were 3,937:1,480 in the southwest, 1,937 around Canso and on Cape Breton Island and 520 around Halifax (in Chezzetcook, for instance, or in Tor Bay [Guysborough Co.] settled by Acadians after 1778). In New Brunswick there were 3,729: 2,056 in the southeast (Memramcook, Petitcodiac, Shediac, Bouctouche, Richibouctou), 1,227 in the northeast (Tracadie, Caraquet, Restigouche) and 446 in the Madawaska region. About 690 lived on Prince Edward Island, around Malpeque in the west, around Rustico in the centre and on Fortune Bay in the west. There were also about 350 on the Magdalen Islands and in the Gaspé, in the Chaleur Bay area in particular.

By 1867, the year of Canadian Confederation, about 44,910 Acadians lived in New Brunswick (twelve times more than in 1803, but representing less than 12 per cent of the population of the province), 32,830 in Nova Scotia (eight times more than in 1803, 8.5 per cent of the total population) and 9,000 on Prince Edward Island. A century later, in 1971, 235,025 Acadians lived in New Brunswick, then representing 37 per cent of the provincial population. Nova Scotia's 80,215 Acadians represented 10.2 per cent of its population in 1971. On Prince Edward Island, ethnic Acadians in 1971 numbered 15,325, 13.7 per cent of the total.

Although some ethnic Acadians, particularly in Nova Scotia and on Prince Edward Island are no longer French-speaking, we can estimate that Acadians and francophones today make up about 20 per cent of the population of the Maritimes. This proportion is expected to remain relatively stable, as large families are a reality of the past.

It would be more than a century after their return before Acadians would enjoy a minimum of rights and obtain what they were entitled to as equal citizens. They could not own land before 1763. Nova Scotia's Acadians received the right to vote in 1789, but New Brunswick's Acadians could not vote until 1810, and those on Prince Edward Island had to wait until 1830. After 1830, Acadians could become members of all three provincial legislatures—where the use of French was unrecognized at the time—but old prejudices still remained. When Simon d'Entremont of Pubnico, first Acadian MLA in Nova Scotia, elected in 1836, was requested to take a "big oath" of allegiance to the king instead of the ordinary oath, he replied: "I'd rather swallow a dogfish tail first than swear to that."

HENRI-DOMINIQUE PARATTE

Acadian pioneer village, Mont-Carmel, P.E.I.

Of the 8,000 to 10,000 Acadians deported from the Maritime provinces, three-quarters had ended up in the American colonies or been put in jail in Halifax or London. The rest had hidden in the woods of New Brunswick or walked to Canada. After the colonial wars were over, Acadians had to find new land and create permanent settlements before they could reorganize on a larger scale. It was not easy.

For a long time the uncertainty remained. When, for instance, Acadians living at Sainte-Anne (now Fredericton) faced the influx of Loyalists who had left the United States, they had to leave their homes. Although they had been there for fifteen years, the Acadians had no titles to the land. This "second expulsion" became in 1975 the subject of a play by Acadian playwright Jules Boudreau, *Cochu et le soleil* (Cochu and the sun): Cochu is forced by Loyalists to leave his land and out of rage he burns the house he had built. The Acadians of Sainte-Anne may not have burned their homes. A few negotiated some form of settlement with the new English settlers. Some went south to Memramcook, others went north along the Saint John River and finally arrived at Saint-Basile, where they were granted title to lots of 200 acres per family.

In the Memramcook Valley, a pleasant and fertile agricultural region, Acadians tried to recreate the life they had known before the Expulsion. In 1765 a small group of refugees from Fort Beauséjour came to that region, which had already been dyked by Acadians, and settled on the west side of the river. They were joined in 1770 by Acadians who had been prisoners for 12 years at Fort Edward at Pisiquid, now Windsor. Most of the latter settled on the west bank, some on the east—Landry, Richard, Breau, Leblanc, Comeau, Dupuis and Bourgeois.

In 1781 the first parish to be established after the Expulsion was created at Memramcook. The previous year, however, British families had moved into the lower part of the valley, taking the richest dykelands on the east bank for themselves. With the creation of New Brunswick in 1784, they joined with Acadians in reclaiming the lands of a major absentee landlord, Bulkley, and were granted 38 lots in 1786. Acadians also obtained British titles to their lands shortly thereafter, but although they were ten times as many as the English, they got lots of poorer quality and only 27 of them.

On the west bank things went less smoothly. Acadians were victimized by Mary Cannon, the mistress of the landowner, a member of the DesBarres family. Despite their numbers, Acadians had to work as tenants for a hostile owner. From 1793 to 1794 climatic conditions created a famine, and a number of Acadians chose to leave. In 1797, Acadians declared that DesBarres did not have a valid claim to the land, and they refused to pay rent. By 1800 all Acadians had united against DesBarres. British soldiers asked them again to swear the oath of allegiance (50 years after the Expulsion, and although they were now British citizens) and threatened them with imprisonment inside Fort Beauséjour. Many Acadians left their lands and moved, if only to the other bank. In 1802, courts recognized the DesBarres' title, and Acadians who did not want to pay back six years of rent were kicked out. It took Acadians 50 years to settle matters with the DesBarres family.

Some Acadians of Memramcook were able to remain where they

Shipbuilding, c. 1870.

had come to resettle. This was not the case everywhere. On Prince Edward Island, Acadians held progressively less and less land as they were pushed away by English landowners. Under the French regime, most Acadians on the island had been both fishermen and farmers. They had been deported in 1758 and some had come back to extremely hard conditions. In 1764, Samuel Holland described the few families he saw as poor, living in tiny cottages in the woods and eating fish and game. In 1768 the 200 Acadians on the island worked for British fish companies.

In 1798, Acadian families were present at Malpeque, Rustico and Baie-de-Fortune on Prince Edward Island, and most were related in some way. They were still viewed as potential traitors by the British and had to accept a tenants' status in order to farm. The land on the island had been conceded to British absentee landowners who were required to find settlers of Protestant stock. Many Acadians cleared the land, but, not being Protestant, had to move once they had done so. Others who farmed were evicted under the pretext that their claims were not valid.

Near Chéticamp, Nova Scotia.

Despite the fact that Acadians around Baie-de-Fortune had received titles from a British naval officer in 1764, the agent of lot 43 claimed rent from them. Between 1786 and 1787 many of these Acadians moved to Chéticamp on Cape Breton Island where it was easier to obtain land from the Crown. Despite official confirmation of their claims by the governor, others on Prince Edward Island discovered that the London Board of Trade did not recognize their titles. Despite the fact that Loyalists received their lands for free, the British insisted that Acadians had to rent or buy it. Most of these Acadians ended up moving to Cape Breton or to other parts of P.E.I. Acadians at Chezzetcook and Grand Désert in central Nova Scotia had difficulty receiving titles to their land and their lots were usually smaller than those of other groups. The same story continued until the 1860s.

Poor, without much formal education and without much idea of their legal status, Acadians tried to find land where they could live without being tenants or threatened with eviction at every turn. This explains why they finally settled land far from major English centres, and why Acadian regions, even today, are marked by a fierce regional spirit. To Acadians, the region they fought so hard to settle in is the centre of their world, and they rarely feel part of a broader com-

The church at Tignish, P.E.I.

munity, in which they would be simply another ethnic group.

Such independence had two sides. One was positive, tending to preserve the community's identity, language and traditions. The other side was negative: members of communities tended to intermarry more than is advisable, relations between the various members became fixed and hard to change, and new influences were systematically countered, leading Acadians to appear as a backward group. In 1870 an Acadian from Tignish, writing in the *Summerside Journal*, noted how necessary it was to change, to have lawyers and businessmen and engineers and to catch up with other groups on the island, but the question was: how?

The first hundred years after the Expulsion was a time of reorganization in the Maritimes. Acadians had to resettle and this took time and hard work, even when there was no risk of being evicted again. When Joseph Dugas travelled on a Mi'kmaq path crossing two rivers to reach L'Anse-des-Leblanc on Saint Mary's Bay in September 1768 with his wife and small daughter, the first thing he did was build a rough hut covered with "machequoui" (birchboard). Around the same time, Acadians who had come back to Memramcook from Massachusetts, and had been turned away roughly from the Port Royal area, joined the group. In the 1770s they were granted lands on the condition that they would build a house, clear land and grow flax.

Women were as strong-willed as men. Madeleine à Pierre LeBlanc, having come from Salem, Massachusetts, to what is now Pointe-de l'église (Church Point), took axe in hand to overcome the depressed mood of her parents and friends who, having lost everything, now faced the "primeval forest" sung by Longfellow. She lived to be 98 and had many children, continued to encourage all, ending each of the many stories she had to tell with: "poverty never killed anyone." It may not have been true, but it gave heart to Baie-Sainte-Marie Acadians who now found themselves forced to become fishermen, sea traders, loggers, home builders, farmers, hunters and anything they could to get by.

To experience the feeling of what Acadian life was like in those days, one would need to contemplate every region because every village was different and very often even language differed from place to place. Although it may sometimes be felt today that Acadian regionalism is detrimental to the collective purpose of building a strong Acadian community, a look back will clearly indicate that the basis of everything in Acadie, from culture to livelihood, has its origin in the local and regional community, not in any abstract idea of what Acadie should be. Acadie is, first of all, how Acadians lived their lives in the places where they were finally allowed to live.

The 1880s brought a major change as Acadian society started to view itself as not just a gathering of communities, but as a group with a collective will. Acadian conventions which began in 1881, deeply influenced the development of Acadie until the 1950s. People who were essentially self-sufficient or considered cheap labour found that strength resided in unity. They also discovered that the resistance of governments and of the anglophone community was far greater than they had expected.

HENRI-DOMINIQUE PARATTE

Spinning at the Acadian Historical Village.

For the first fifty years after the Deportation, Acadian elites had been small and parochial, save for a few people such as Joseph Guegen (1741-1825), founder of Cocagne, New Brunswick, who had the ability to read, write and communicate with British authorities. From the mid-nineteenth century, such parochialism was useless in the development of a common Franco-Acadian identity. Acadians need competent people in all fields, control of the institutions that ruled their lives, and respect for their rights from authorities. These needs have formed the basis for major developments in Acadie over the past hundred years.

Anyone in contact with Québécois or Acadians will at one point or another hear mention of "La Patente." Under the official title of

L'Ordre de Jacques-Cartier, this group, founded in Ontario in 1926, sought to advance the cause of French Canadians wherever it could and functioned as a kind of old boys' network that worked discreetly until 1965. It was created to counter the hold that anglophone old boys' networks had on certain functions. For example some anglophone families, such as the Odell family in New Brunswick for a long time had an apparent monopoly on power in their province; the same was true at many other levels including federal politics, as Alexandre Boudreau (probably the first Acadian to be Canada's General Consul in Boston) pointed out in his memoirs À l'assaut des défis in 1984.

Acadians could not take anything for granted. Even within the Catholic Church they had to struggle to be recognized. It took some time for priests to respond to their needs, and it took until the early twentieth century to shake the strongly anti-Acadian church establishment controlled by Irish and Scottish bishops in the Maritimes, and to obtain their first Acadian bishop.

There had been a few Acadian priests before the Expulsion. The first, Bernardin de Falaise, born at Port Royal in 1704, was ordained a Récollet friar, and his brother Pierre became canon of the cathedral in Quebec City. In the wake of the Expulsion, there were few priests and no Acadian parishes left as such. Acadians were served mostly by priests from Quebec until 1817. Mathurin Bourg, born at Rivière-aux-Canards in 1744, was deported to Virginia with his family in 1755. He went to England and then to France to study after 1763, was ordained in 1772 and came back to Acadie the following year. From 1774 to 1795 he served as the vicar-general of missions in Acadie and his influence over the Mi'kmaq helped to keep them neutral during the war of U.S. independence. Other Acadian priests followed. For example, Ephrem-Sylvain Poirier from Prince Edward Island was ordained in 1828. Priests from France and Quebec stayed and supported the Acadian revival of the late 19th century.

The church was not just a spiritual force. It was in many ways the only organized administration. People thought in terms of villages, of course, but also of parishes. In France until the Revolution, like in Acadie, there had been no record of births, but records of christenings had been kept. Acadian regions in Louisiana today are still referred to as parishes.

At a time when administration in Halifax or elsewhere was in English only, the presence of priests who could read and write French was essential to Acadians in their struggling and isolated communities. They provided the basic means for Acadians to communicate with others who had survived the Expulsion and came back and

Saint Mary's church at Church Point, Nova Scotia.
It is the tallest wooden spire in North America. In the background
are the old buildings of l'Université Sainte-Anne.

started anew. Everyone went by the calendar of the Church, with its feasts, periods of fasting and annual celebrations.

Before Acadian communities were able to obtain a priest, a missionary would normally visit them once or twice a year, but sometimes longer periods went by. No missionaries went to Prince Edward Island from 1785 to 1790. Laymen presided over burials and messes blanches (masses without a priest) and taught what they could. Each region erected its chapel and a little rectory and gave one twenty-sixth of its potatoes to the missionary. On the whole the Catholic Church was an important element in the rebuilding of an Acadian identity, for better and for worse.

ACADIAN HISTORICAL VILLAGE

Légère's blacksmith shop, c. 1836.

How should we imagine these Acadians? They were strong-willed, fiercely independent, but also rather destitute. We can imagine them in houses like the simple Maison Martin, now in the Village Historique Acadien (Acadian Historical Village) opened in 1977 near Caraquet, N.B., a sturdy "pièces sur pièces" construction of squared logs fastened with wooden pegs to uprights 2 metres apart, cracks filled with moss and mud, a shingled roof, white plaster covering the whole construction, no floor, the simplest of fireplaces, no loft and a few shelves. Acadians visiting the Village Historique for the first time are often shocked by the level of poverty this meant. Little by little, houses became larger and more comfortable, like the Savoie House of

The Savoie house, c. 1870.

the 1860s, with its summer kitchen. Fireplaces were replaced by stoves and shingles came to be manufactured. Farms had more barns and the family of every fisherman came to have a small shed to keep firewood and to salt the fish.

Anyone visiting the Village Historique cannot fail to observe the difference between the Acadian houses, limited in their design and size by financial constraints, and the houses of the Anglo-Protestant elite, such as the Blackhall traders who came to Caraquet in 1822. Acadians of the past must have also been aware of the social differences that took so long to overcome. And there were undoubtedly differences among Acadians themselves, from the *sagouines* at the bottom of the ladder to the small elite at the top, right below the anglophone elite, where there was one. However, without a strong feeling that all Acadians could band together to claim when they were entitled to, no progress would have been made towards achieving the collective goals that form the basis of today's Acadie.

II. Gaining Rights and Collective Goals

Several elements help to ensure the continued growth and development of a community: symbols of identity, political presence, schooling adapted to the needs of the community, and communications. When a group faces the many problems of being a minority, these elements are even more essential.

In 1880 the Société Saint-Jean-Baptiste of Quebec invited some Acadians to attend their congress. Forty attended and decided to organize an Acadian convention. The following year, 5,000 gathered in Memramcook to talk about education, agriculture, forced emigration to other parts of Canada or the United States, the possibility of opening new villages and the choice of a "national" day. The date chosen was August 15, the time of the celebration of the Blessed Virgin.

A second convention took place in Miscouche in 1884, where the red, white and blue flag with a gold star was adopted and "Ave Maris Stella" ("Hail, Star of the Sea") was chosen as the national anthem. Again the questions of fighting emigration to the States (where a large number of young Acadians, male and female, went to earn better wages in the factories) and of opening new rural parishes (a basic idea of the Catholic establishment in French Canada at that time) were discussed at length.

Now that Acadians felt more like a community they were able to move on to other goals. Their leaders, often priests, were largely religious and conservative people, but no progress would have been made without them at a time when schooling for most Acadians was limited and often in English. In 1890 at Pointe-de-l'église the request was for more use of the French language in schools. In 1900 at Arichat, Nova Scotia, in the presence of Canadian prime minister Wilfrid Laurier, the main topics were the needs to have an Acadian bishop and to have newspapers that would serve the community better and rely more on Acadian topics and journalists. In 1905 at Caraquet and in 1908 at Saint-Basile the same requests were made again, as well as requests for some teaching of French in teachers' colleges in the Maritimes and for French textbooks in Acadian schools. It was also suggested that Acadians should become more involved in business and trade.

A bishop having been named, the 1913 Tignish convention expressed its thanks, while drawing up plans to bring Acadians who had left for New England back to the Maritimes. In 1921 at Pointe-de l'église, Acadians decided to revive the memories of Grand Pré, where the Société Nationale l'Assomption had acquired some land, and expressed a desire to see a memorial church there. This church, built in 1923, became the nucleus of the present historic site, which celebrates Acadian identity. The convention also called for gross mistakes about Acadian history to be eradicated from textbooks for schools.

Conventions grew more and more complex and became like an unofficial Acadian parliament. In 1927 at Moncton a whole political and economic program was put together, with the goals of better representation within the government of New Brunswick and of being more adequately served by cooperatives in agriculture, the fisheries, lumber trading and industrial ventures. Acadians were invited to request some knowledge of French by the federal and provincial civil servants who were supposed to serve them. From convention to convention, similar themes returned again and again, proving not only that Acadians knew what they wanted but that governments were slow in responding and that important plans took time.

At Memramcook in 1937, fisheries, newspapers and school rights were up for discussion again. This convention was followed in 1955 by the celebrations for the bicentennial of the Acadian Expulsion.

The Société Nationale l'Assomption had been founded at Memramcook in 1881 and organized congresses regularly until 1955. As times changed it adopted a different mandate and a new name. Laymen slowly replaced priests in positions of responsibility. In 1957 it became the Société Nationale des Acadiens (SNA), as a joint organization representing Acadian organizations in all three Maritime provinces, with a permanent secretariat in Moncton at first, then in Shédiac, now in Dieppe. Its 1960 convention recommended the creation of an Acadian university in Moncton. Today, to recognize the equality of men and women (Acadien being a masculine form) it is called Société Nationale de l'Acadie, dealing primarily with national and international reprepsentation of the Acadian community.

Acadians gathered in Caraquet in 1965 to recognize the special needs of young people and the urgency of keeping up with events affecting them. By then, it was becoming obvious that Acadians from the three Maritime provinces did not share the same preoccupations on all topics, their potential rate of growth and development was not the same and their numbers called for different strategies.

The 1972 Fredericton convention, attended by more than 1,000 delegates, voted on 264 motions in all fields and was also the start of the organization that now represents Acadians in New Brunswick, the Société des Acadiens du Nouveau-Brunswick (SANB) (now called

Société des Acadiens et Acadiennes du Nouveau-Brunswick). Founded in Shippagan in 1973, it created a major debate when it moved from Moncton to Petit-Rocher a few years later. Although the northern coast had been the most solidly French-speaking part of eastern New Brunswick, Acadian institutions had generally grown in the southeast, which had a greater population of Acadians, more often mixed with English. It was not the only institution to move, and these movements have revitalized the northeast, a region long forgotten by governments and which has faced high levels of poverty, unemployment and emigration despite the fact that Caraquet calls itself "la capitale de l'Acadie" and that the region is one of the main fishing centers in the Maritimes.

In 1979, New Brunswick Acadians organized another convention in Edmundston where one thousand representatives from all parishes in the province supported the ideas of autonomy for Acadian regions and decentralization of government offices. Although most of the delegates were professionals already supporting the Parti Acadien the convention sent a clear message to politicians that Acadians wanted action and were not willing to accept anglicization as the solution to their problems. It also sent the clear signal that Acadians had different goals in their

MARTINE JACQUOT

respective provinces and that cooperation rather than unanimity was the order of the day. Anyone there who heard the crowd sing "Réveil"—a song created by Louisiana Cajun Zachary Richard—to conclude celebrations cannot forget how intense collective feeling was at that time. It did not die or wither away. This spirit was gradually transformed into programs, structural changes and plans of action that would enable Acadians to become full citizens of the Maritime community including equality of francophones and anglophones in New Brunswick, and the right to education in French, as official rights recognized by the constitution of Canada.

The SNA was led for most of the 1980s by Léger Comeau and Jean-Marie Nadeau (a former editor of *L'Acayen* magazine who would go from the SNA to work as editor for the daily newspaper *L'Acadie Nouvelle* for a few years before becoming active in the newly revived labor movement in the 1990s.) Both were aware that Acadians in different provinces had different needs and both believed the SNA should represent all Acadians with an opening towards the world. The SNA now had a different mission. It had included organizations from the three provinces, but 1986 saw its mandate broadened to national and international representation, an important element at a time when francophone summits were starting, and with a Canadian prime minister, Brian Mulroney, who had written some years earlier that "top Quebecers, francophone Ontarians, and Acadians should be sought out for major leadership roles. The traditional roles of 'assistant to,' 'deputy of,' and 'second vice-president' no longer suffice." Such a statement could be endorsed by Jean Chrétien, the present prime minister of Canada who was first elected in Bouctouche when he came back to politics. The SNA in 1998 was presided over by Liane Roy, with René Légère as its director.

The discussion unifying the three Maritime Provinces that was carried on during the 1970s did not enjoy much support from Acadians, who felt that they had been forgotten in all Canadian constitutional talks in the past, and that the union of three provinces so economically tied to New England would ruin most of what they had accomplished over the past century. They understood better than ever that ownership of communications networks and school systems in their own language were essential for the development of Acadian communities. Cooperation between provinces, however, was largely encouraged.

In the 1970s many Acadians, particularly young professionals, felt that the time had come to recreate an Acadie that would be their own. Some thought about a province, and some, such as novelist Claude Le Bouthillier, even thought about forming a country, as in the novel *L'Acadien reprend son pays* (Getting back an Acadian country). The idea was that, should there be any attempt at unifying the three Maritime provinces, an Acadian province with a common border with Quebec should also be created. This showed clearly that inventive administrative changes were needed to accomodate Acadian reality.

Francophones in the Maritimes recognized that no city in the region would ever offer them the opportunities to be found in Montreal. Sociologists have noted for quite a while that Montreal has

Novelist Claude Le Bouthillier.

increasingly become an important city for Acadians. Direct flights from Moncton to Montreal are one of many examples. Acadians however, wanted a future in the Maritimes, not in Quebec. Acadians had by the 1970s begun to think about their collective future, not as a unit led by a few leaders singing the same tune, but as a group with many points of view and abilities to express them.

III. Communications: Necessary Tools

Communications enable any community to know itself and its needs. For Harold Innis, the fall of the Roman Empire could be attributed to a breakdown in communications from one end of the empire to the other. The other side of the coin is economy. Gaps in communications and insufficient wealth may lead a community, however big and powerful, to self-destruct gradually. When a community has suffered from poor education, isolated settlements and the overwhelming presence of another culture around it, communications become even more important. Acadie might have disappeared had its people not found ways to create their own communications networks.

Before the Acadian revival of the 1880s, oral culture played an essential role. Songs, for example, told stories about contemporary events, poked fun at individuals, recounted journeys to logging camps in Canada or expressed the difficulties of emigrating to the States. Oral culture included everything from gossip to long stories about one's own or other communities. It was expressed in Acadian French, which kept traits of the French spoken in Poitou and other regions when settlers had come to Acadie, blending them with new words, sometimes borrowed from English or Mi'kmaq.

In contrast, the language the priests spoke, particularly in their official functions, was a more standard French, and no trace of Acadian French can be found in the published speeches from the first three Acadian conventions.

Acadians needed communications systems more adapted to the time in the 1900s. Newspapers were then the only communications tool that could reach a large audience. *Le Moniteur Acadien*, a rather conservative newspaper, but a major milestone in the expression of ideas directed towards the whole Acadian community, was first published in Shediac by Israel Landry in 1867. It had a rocky career and stopped publication for financial reasons soon after it began. Bought by Norbert Lussier in 1868, it was published until 1871. Fernand Robidoux then bought it and it came out until 1918. It then disappeared for six years, surfaced again for two and disappeared altogether in 1926.

Le Courrier des Provinces Maritimes was founded in Bathurst in 1885 and, although its history was as rocky as that of *Le Moniteur Acadien*, the personalities around it are fascinating. Owned by Valentin Landry from 1884 to 1887, it was directed by Pierre-Jean Veniot from 1894 to 1900.

Born in 1844 at Pokemouche, New Brunswick, Valentin Landry had studied at Truro and been a primary school teacher and a school director in Nova Scotia before becoming the first Acadian school inspector in New Brunswick in 1879. He then left New Brunswick to found a new weekly, *L'Evangéline*, in Digby, Nova Scotia. It would become the longest-living Acadian newspaper. Later on this paper moved to Weymouth, and then to Moncton in 1905. Valentin Landry remained its manager until 1910, and he died in 1919. *L'Evangéline* survived, becoming the only Acadian daily in 1949, until it finally went into receivership and disappeared altogether in 1982.

Pierre-Jean Veniot, born in Richibouctou in 1863, studied at Pictou Academy before working in Moncton for the *Transcript*. After years with *Le Courrier des Provinces Maritimes*, he started a political career and became the Liberal MLA for Gloucester from 1894 to 1900 and 1917 to 1923. Minister of public works for New Brunswick from 1919 to 1923, he was elected leader to reorganize the party in 1923 and thus became the first Acadian premier of New Brunswick—quite a feat when we look back at where Acadians were one century earlier. A staunch defender of Maritime rights, Veniot promoted the notion of public ownership of the provincial hydro system. After being defeated provincially in 1925, he was elected to the Canadian House of Commons for Gloucester, where he served from 1926 to 1936, during which time among other functions, he was postmaster general for four years. He decided that Canadian stamps should carry both French and English just as we know them today. He died in 1936. Veniot had proven that Acadians were to be reckoned with in the Maritimes and Canada, that they were important for the francophone community as a whole and that their presence could be important for political parties in New Brunswick and Canada.

The newspaper Landry and Veniot worked for together was not as lucky as they were. It tried hard to promote the awakening of Acadians culturally, economically and politically, but competition and other factors including the liberal tendencies of the editors, led to its disappearance twice, in 1886 and 1898. Its demise was in a way less important than the message that it had carried and the people it had led to advance Acadian politics and journalism.

L'Evangéline survived in its last years thanks to material support from France and financial support from various Acadian institutions. It was closed because of conflicts between employees and a staunchly "elitist" management, because its main readership was in northeastern New Brunswick and on the Acadian peninsula while editorial work was done in Moncton, and because of its difficulty in making a profit.

Replacing a 96-year-old newspaper with admittedly nationalist goals was far from easy. Facing increased pressures from a more adequately funded English media, something had to be done to give Acadians a way to communicate in New Brunswick and in the Maritime region as a whole. In 1984 a group of private business people from the Acadian peninsula founded, in Caraquet, *L'Acadie*

Nouvelle, a regional daily. However, they did not have the financial means to distribute it to other regions on a daily basis. Meanwhile a group of representatives from Acadian institutions obtained support from the New Brunswick government and private businesses to launch *Le Matin* in 1986 from Moncton as a provincial newspaper, which later died a difficult death in 1988.

Both dailies then had about 8,000 subscribers, both had financial problems, their joint network covered most of New Brunswick, but merger attempts failed. *L'Acadie Nouvelle* now receives enough

MARTINE JACQUOT

The first offices of l'Acadie Nouvelle, *Caraquet.*
The building, a historical landmark, has since been destroyed by fire.

support from a public trust fund to flourish as the provincial French daily for New Brunswick and its readership has grown with increasingly modern managements. Why public support? The answer is simple: in a province where the Irving conglomerate controls most of the anglophone media, the only alternative to public funding would have been Quebec or Ontario press ownership—a situation potentially detrimental to Acadian pride and Maritime interests.

The bitter regional political and personal undertones the fight between the two dailies brought into the open made it clear that, as the Acadian community matured, regional concerns were becoming sometimes more important than the abstract ideal of general consensus. The Acadian community had given itself nationalist goals from the 1880s but had recognized from the 1960s how different Acadian communities in the three Maritime provinces were. It now had to recognize that regions inside those provinces had diverging interests, and that Acadie as a whole could not exist if any of its regions was not considered or faced serious underdevelopment.

Acadians also had to face the fact that they were scattered across huge distances. *L'Evangéline* had never reached the Madawaska on time to be of real interest, largely because it was produced in Moncton. *L'Acadie Nouvelle* is at least more in the middle of Acadian regions in New Brunswick.

Newspapers were not limited to New Brunswick. *L' Impartial* appeared in Prince Edward Island in 1895, thanks to Gilbert Buote and his son François, and was published until 1915. Since 1976, *La Voix Acadienne* has served the weekly needs of Acadian readers on the island. *Le Petit Courrier*, a weekly published in Nova Scotia in 1937 by Désiré d'Eon and known as the porte-patchets (door-to-door news salesman) became the provincial Acadian weekly *Le Courrier* in 1972. After owner Cyrille Leblanc sold *Le Courrier*, it passed into the hands of a special provincial Acadian "press group" in 1988. Its 60th anniversary was a major cause of celebration, particularly in West Pubnico, Nova Scotia.

In northwestern New Brunswick, *Le Madawaska*, a weekly newspaper founded in Edmundston in 1913 by Albert Sormany and Maximilien Cormier, now has nearly 7,000 subscribers. Nearby Grand-Sault (Grand Falls) is served by *La Cataracte*, a bilingual weekly. All regions are served by a least one weekly paper. *L'Aviron* was founded in Caraquet in 1965 by Corinne Blanchard (1905-73), a woman journalist who had worked for *L'Evangéline* for several years, became biweekly in 1984, joining forces with *Le Point* in Bathurst. *Le Voilier* is published in Carleton

Le Madelinot, the bi-monthly of the Magdalen Islands, founded in 1965, was replaced by *Le Radar*. In southeastern New Brunswick, after several ill-fated attempts, *Le Moniteur* and *ProKent* became regular weeklies in the 1980s. Of course, the smaller bulletins of parishes and Acadian societies still convey a lot of basic information.

Among the weeklies that were created in the late 1990s *Le Journal* in Dieppe, proved one of the best with an Acadian editorial team...and the backing of Irving money, but disappeared after six

L'Acadie NOUVELLE

LE QUOTIDIEN DES FRANCOPHONES DU N.-B.

SOMMAIRE

LE VENDREDI 8 AOUT 1997   14ᵉ année   ÉDITION 3319

75 ¢ + TVH   88 pages

29e Gala de la chanson de Caraquet

MICHELLE BOUDREAU SAMSON TRIOMPHE!

pages 2 et 3

Concept 2001 junior

RÉGIONAL

Dundee garde aussi son école

page 18

RÉGIONAL

Moncton: l'eau est à nouveau potable

page 8

SPORTS

Junior AAA: c'est parti à Moncton

pages 62 et 63

SPORTS

Marc Goguen vise la victoire à Cocagne

page 61

Aidez votre enfant à prendre son envol avec le dernier-né de nos produits d'assurance.

Téléphonez: 1-800-455-7337

Assomption Vie
Au coeur de votre avenir

A recent front page, L'Acadie Nouvelle *newspaper*

months. Others like *Express Chaleur* or *Le Noroît,* started publishing in the northeast. Life is never easy for Acadian media but their very numbers are proof of the cultural dynamism of the population.

Journalists in Acadian written media are poorly paid compared to any other French-speaking area. This may in part explain the labour-management difficulties some newspapers have faced. Lack of capital also explains the fact that there are few Acadian magazines.

After the short life of *L'Acayen* magazine (linked with the Parti Acadien, the only party that publicly called for an Acadian province in the 1980s) and of the Moncton arts magazine *Rézo*, an Acadian magazine was finally launched successfully by Euclide Chiasson and a team of dedicated correspondents in 1985 as *Ven' d'est*. Bruno Godin, Loic Venin, Martin Pitre, Michel Saint-Onge are among the many who developed it into a quarterly offering information and views on all parts of Acadie and various other topics. Euclide Chiasson, born in 1944, taught philosophy before becoming involved in community development work, helped to found the Parti Acadien and served as its first president from 1972 to 1975, and represented a forestry union from 1981 to 1984 before founding *le Ven d'est*. He now works in the co-op movement for the Atlantic region. Various magazines appeared and disappeared in the late 1980s: *Infomag, TV Atlantique,* and *Pleins Feux*. The New Brunswick Acadian artists association (AAAPNB) now publishes the quarterly *Idéarts*, on artistic development, and the international association of Acadian families publishes *Retrouvailles*, a historical quarterly.

The late 1970s saw the publication of many journals with limited circulation but with literary, social or political importance, from academic journals such as *Si Que* (meaning "If" in Acadian French) and *La Revue de l' Université de Moncton* to literary magazines such as *Eloizes* (meaning "Bolt of lightning" in Acadian French) and political magazines such as *Egalité*. Although they do not reach the larger mass of Acadians, ideas expressed in these publications are discussed by a growing middle class increasingly conscious of its importance as the numbers of the older elite and clergy dwindle. *Eloizes* is also a welcome link with other areas where writers write in French: Louisiana and Ontario, for instance.

Young Acadian journalists can learn their trade at their own publications, and they do not have to go to Quebec, Ontario or anglophone universities any longer to get started. Université de Moncton now offers a program in communications in French.

Acadians have sought to provide themselves with a clear vision of their communities that will clearly define an Acadian space for the younger generations and overcome the constant threat of anglicization especially in more isolated Acadian communities. If newspapers were a means of communication adapted to the 1900s, the same way oral tales were important in the 1800s, in the 1950s the presence of powerful electronic media to the south called for an electronic environment in which Acadians could find their place. Acadians still had no central town of their own. Moncton came the closest because of numbers and institutions, but Caraquet felt it was the true capital. Meanwhile the whole community was moving away from the culture of villages to the McLuhanesque culture of the global village. What could Acadians do?

Once again, some of their leaders had long-term plans and sought public support for them. Leaders of the 1950s such as Father Clément Cormier, the first president of Université de Moncton in 1963, and nationalist Senator Calixte Savoie asked the Société Radio-Canada (the French side of CBC) to take Acadian interests into account. They

VEN' D'EST

Euclide Chiasson.

were keenly aware that, for a population still deficient in secondary and advanced schooling in its own language, the lack of francophone media adapted to its particular interests would be a major disaster. Regional disparity would become worse, and Acadians would once again become second-class citizens in all three Maritime provinces.

At the end of the 1950s, there still was no French radio or television network to act as the counterpart of ATV in English. Acadians in northeastern New Brunswick could listen to French radio stations coming from Quebec (CHNC New Carlisle); francophones in the Madawaska to a local station CJEM, founded in 1944, and several stations from Quebec. But in the early 1970s Radio-Canada, present in southeastern New Brunswick since 1954, did not adequately serve the northern part of the same province and served with difficulty Acadians in other provinces. Listening to CBC, ATV or other anglophone channels as many did, was enough to convince any young Acadian that Acadie was only present in his or her village, and that most of it was either folklore or history—a history that no media talked about and of which schools taught very little!

By the mid-1970s the Société Radio-Canada, under the influence of major Acadian figures like managers Laetitia Cyr or Claude Bourque realized that its mandate to serve Acadians was not to feed them programs from Quebec, however good and interesting those were, but to help Acadian creators, journalists and technicians to develop their skills and reach their own markets. Local production for the Maritimes in Moncton was gradually increased, starting with news programming and expanding into several programs of folk music, country music, rock, cultural information and Acadian movies. Broadcasts such as "Encore debout" (a title taken from a song by Calixte Duguay), "Pistroli" (an Acadian word meaning "frolic"), "Chez Angèle" and others gave Acadian creators the opportunity to perform. A country music program produced from Moncton became the most widely viewed program in French Canada. Acadian events were covered more consistently by national TV programs like "Les Beaux Dimanches." RFI, the French newsworld channel, covers Acadian reality constantly with a growing base of young Acadian journalists. "Ce soir," on the first TV channel of the S.R.C., offers a complete survey of events affecting Acadians every night.

Radio programming was increased more than television programming primarily because it was less expensive. Afternoon programs were tried for Prince Edward Island ("La Marée de l'Ile" [Island Tide]) and for Nova Scotia ("A marée haute" [High Tide] in the 1980s, and in 1986 the morning news program "Bonjour Atlantique," a three-hour broadcast involving regional correspondents and covering all aspects of Acadian reality, was divided into three, one for each province. The Nova Scotia program was produced from Halifax, the result of years of pressure upon Radio-Canada by that province's Acadian and francophone community. Its original director, Jules Chiasson, is now directing all French radio programming in Moncton.

Commercial radio stations took a number of listeners from Radio-Canada, particularly CJVA in Caraquet, founded in 1977. The trend in the 1980s has been to give communities a view of themselves, with the creation of a network of community radio stations. The year 1989 saw the birth of four amidst financial difficulties and much effort by volunteers—on the Magdalen Islands, at Baie Sainte-Marie, in Madawaska and on the Acadian peninsula. The radio station at Université de Moncton acts as a community network. A radio station like CIFA is doing a lot to boost pride among Acadians in southwest Nova Scotia. Other stations are now developing in Chéticamp and in Dieppe.

At Radio-Clare, Dave LeBlanc and Jean-Louis Belliveau
advertise CIFA in November 1997.

In and around Moncton, where 40 per cent of viewers were francophones, Acadian organizations pushed the cable television service to offer TVA, a Quebec channel, in 1988. In 1989 an international French network, a direct result of the francophone summits, TV5, was added, bringing the number of French channels available in that part of New Brunswick to seven out of thirty-two. In Halifax-Dartmouth the francophone community has access to TV5. In the Baie Sainte-Marie, the company Le Cable de la Baie offers Télé Quatre-Saisons and may offer TV5. Other regions should follow, although what is offered often depends on the vagaries of cable systems, space available, and individual will.

An "electronic province" in French, with growing exchanges between radio, computers, telephone systems and satellite networks may provide the basis of a thrilling and complex existence and be one answer to the fundamental question for Acadie of how to serve a population that is largely rural, dispersed and challenged by the anglophone media. Developments on the "electronic highway" are now made in Edmunston, at the CIDIF, a branch of the Université de Moncton developing software and web strategies in French, but the growing number of websites about Acadians and websites in French in the Maritimes is proof enough that Acadians consider it an important resource for the future.

There are a good number of Web sites today relating to Acadians, not only for historical reasons, but also because of tourism, major events, and the overall development of new media.

There is also a CD-Rom just developed by a Cape Breton company, Portage Technologies, offering a multimedia history under the title *L'Acadie CD-Rom.* It will be followed at the end of 1998 with a CD-Rom on the Cajuns of Louisiana. The site of the company can be accessed at http://www.portageinc.com

Several sites can be accessed from Daniel Robichaud's site called "L'Acadie au bout des doigts" (Acadie at your fingertips) at http://www.rpa.ca/acadie/. It covers primarily New Brunswick, but offers many links with the francophone world, numerous local sites in New Brunswick, and tourist attractions, usually both in English and in French.

The Centre d'Etudes Acadiennes at the Université de Moncton offers numerous documents on their site, covering history and folklore in particular, including Acadian traditional songs available on-line.

The Centre Acadien at Université Sainte-Anne offers a site called L'Epopée Acadienne, which gives information on genealogy, history, and some aspects of contemporary Acadia (including a link to the play *Evangéline,* performed at Baie Sainte-Marie every summer). It can be accessed at:

http://www.rescol.ca/collections/acadian/english/toce/toce.htm

The best genealogy sites on-line (besides some paying sites) are Francêtres:Acadian genealogy, available at:

http://www.cam.org/~beaur/gen/acadie-e.html

And Geneanet, covering all of francophone North America, at

http: //www.geocities.com/Heartland/Meadows/3699/

Most genealogy sites will offer links to others, so it is likely that, between broad family sites, books and on-line information, everyone can find his or her ancestors from the time Acadie was founded.

Tourist sites will usually include a page about Acadians in English, such as the page offered by Valley-Web as:

http://www.valleyweb.com/acadians/

Information on those pages—as everything on the Web—should be considered unchecked and not always accurate, although it is usually pilfered from books on Acadians without acknowledgement of copyright. If you have to use information from the Web for a class assignment, make sure to double-check the information with more "classical" sources.

Acadian schools often have Web pages these days: one of the first was the elementary school in Petit-de-Grat, Cape Breton:

http://www.franco.ca/education/ecolepdg/

Such pages are a good way to get in touch with an actual, contemporary, Acadian reality.

Saint-Pierre et Miquelon, the small French department near Newfoundland, has a rich and interesting Web page:

http://205.250.151.22/encyspmweb/english.html

It is a good way to get links with the French reality in France, and the francophone realities of Europe, where new Web sites are being created by the hundreds every day, even though French—particularly in France—faced a delay in the development of IT compared to Canada and North America in general.

One of the most interesting developments of IT technology in the Maritimes has been the creation of the CIDIF, a centre at the Edmundston campus of l'université de Moncton to foster developments of IT links and new Web sites in French, not only for New Brunswick, but for all of the francophone world. The CIDIF site also has a number of documents related to the Francophone Summits, including of course the Summit planned for Moncton in 1999.

Among the interesting sites in France related to Acadians, the site of the town of Loudun, from which a number of people emigrated to Acadia, offers among other interesting documents a web site about the annual light and sound show "The Acadian Epic" and an e-mail group called "Les Loudunautes" which functions in English as well as in French. Both, and more, can be accessed at:

http://www/loudun.cg86.fr/

IV. Education: Building for the Future

Education existed before the Expulsion. Priests who were there to teach the principles of the Catholic faith to Indians also taught the pioneers' children. The first seminary in New France was founded in Acadie in 1632 or 1633, before the one established in Quebec City in 1635, and before the first college in New England, Harvard, was founded in 1637. D'Aulnay added two schools in 1641, one for boys,

Indian and white, and one for girls, Indian and white, the latter under the supervision of Madame de Brice. The first student was Mathieu Martin, a name given to the large Acadian school at Dieppe, near Moncton, more than three centuries later. Boys could learn enough to earn a decent living, and most girls learned as they needed to at the time, to be good mothers and housekeepers. Children learned to read, write and count, and they were taught Latin, hymns and basic elements of the Catholic faith. The letters of Vénérande Robichaux, at the end of the 18th century, are proof of the importance of education for an Acadian middle-class at the time.

According to Lionel Groulx, a Québécois historian of the 1930s who wrote a novel about the return of Acadians to the Maritimes, few places in the world at that time had such high literacy rate among their populations. Petitions to governors were signed by many Acadians, at a time when knowing how to sign one's name was often uncommon.

Despite changes in government and destruction of buildings by the British, members of religious orders kept on teaching children during the French regime. A sister of Congrégation des Soeurs de Notre-Dame, founded in Montreal by Marguerite Bourgeois, was sent to Port Royal as a teacher for girls in 1658, and a sister of Filles de la Croix joined her in 1701. Members of male religious orders also came as teachers sent by the Quebec bishop, from Geoffroy in 1686 to Félix Pain (who became Father Félicien in Longfellow's poem) and Patrice René in 1703. The first Acadian priests, Bernardin and René de Gannes de Falaise, were probably pupils of Patrice René. As Acadians moved along the Bay of Fundy, schools were built at Les Mines and Beaubassin, next to the churches.

The hatred some British governors showed towards Catholic priests, hard for us to imagine nowadays unless we think, perhaps, of Northern Ireland, led colonial authorities to concoct schemes whereby French Catholic priests would be replaced by Scottish Protestant ministers so Acadian children would learn English and change religion. Obviously, these schemes, not much different from the colonial views of Lord Durham in Quebec in the 1830s, did not work and the school at Port Royal continued to function until 1755. On Isle Royale, France paid extreme attention to provide school facilities until the end of the French regime in 1758. However, no full buildings survived the systematic destruction ordered by the British.

Had Acadie of old survived, its inhabitants would have had at least as high a degree of instruction as any other English or French Americans. However, we can imagine parents after the Expulsion,

Notre Dame de l'Assomption School and Church, Chéticamp, Nova Scotia. The 100th anniversary of this church was celebrated in 1993.

---

teaching their children at night about the two things they held dearest: their French language and their Catholic faith. But such teaching did not necessarily imply writing or reading. When Father Sigogne conducted a survey among Acadian families in 1798, he found that only 20 per cent could read and write, down from 50 per cent in 1755.

Sigogne used his rectory to educate, encouraged mothers to teach basic reading and writing skills, and brought an itinerant teacher, Louis Brunet, to Petit-Ruisseau in 1815. Sigogne was, like François Ciquart in Saint-Basile, one of the priests that the 1789 revolution had forced to leave France. At a time when Catholic schools were forbidden in Nova Scotia, where laws did not provide for instruction in French for Acadian pupils, it was up to the clergy and itinerant teachers to preserve the flame of French instruction.

After 1815 things became gradually more organized and each parish in New Brunswick hired teachers and found or constructed buildings for school use. A school was begun in Caraquet in 1826, and one opened in Bathurst in 1840. In Néguac, where Othon Robichaud had taught, a parish school opened in 1853, Petit-Rocher 1851, Shippagan 1857—all parishes in New Brunswick slowly provided school instruction. The province had tried to be fair, granting from 1802 a small amount of public assistance for schools, an attitude markedly different from that in Nova Scotia, which banned all French or parochial schools in 1864. On Prince Edward Island, where Father Beaulieu had erected the first school near his church in Rustico in 1816, French was tolerated, and an 1858 report indicated that twenty Acadian schools (out of a total of 218) taught in French for about 700 children.

Such progress was adequate for elementary teaching, but the quality was poor, and when teachers' colleges were created no provision was made to take into account the need for French to be taught as a first language. Anglophone universities provided no instruction in French, and there were no Acadian lawyers or doctors in 1840 and not more than ten Acadian priests, who had to study in Quebec, France or English seminaries because of the lack of adequate structures in the Maritimes. If Acadians wanted to create an elite to lead them into the twentieth century, they had to have institutions of higher learning. Here, again, the only source of manpower resided in the Catholic Church.

The first Acadian college was founded at Memramcook by Father François-Xavier Lafrance in 1854 and called Séminaire Saint-Thomas. Born in Quebec in 1814, Father Lafrance had studied at Saint Andrew's College in Charlottetown and had been the vicar at Rustico and Tracadie (where he had founded a school and, in 1849, a leper house). Transferred to Memramcook, then the richest parish in Acadie, in 1852, he founded a seminary which had to close in 1862 because of financial problems.

Father Camille Lefebvre (1831-95), also from Quebec, picked up where Father Lafrance had left off and reopened the college in 1863 as Collège Saint-Joseph de Memramcook, which would ultimately become Université de Moncton. In 1873 he began the convent of Notre-Dame du Sacré-Coeur for the education of young women, and in 1880 he founded with Mother Léonie the order of Petites Soeurs de la Sainte Famille, women who provided cleaning and other basic services to teaching institutions in Canada and the United States. The order of Notre-Dame also established a convent at Arichat, Nova Scotia, and at Miscouche, P.E.I. in 1864 (which lasted until 1984). The work of Father Lefebvre was of major significance for Acadians. It is no wonder that the Monument Lefebvre at Saint-Joseph de Memramcook is now accompanied by a guided exhibit called "La survivance des Acadiens," (survival of the Acadians).

Officially, the students of the Memramcook college were supposed to become good bilingual citizens. Anglophones strongly opposed French-only instruction. Monsignor Marcel-François Richard, one of the most dynamic leaders of Acadians in the nineteenth century, promoter of the development of agriculture in Kent County and founder of the village of Rogersville in 1869, learned this when he founded the Collège Saint-Louis for young Acadian men in 1874 (a convent also being opened for young women) to develop not only instruction in French but to defend the Catholic faith and promote the arts and sciences. Under heavy attack from Bishop Rogers of Chatham, the college had to close its doors in 1882.

New Brunswick had until the Common School Act in New Brunswick (1871) been quite open to instruction in French which relied upon Catholic staff. Making all schools public eliminated overnight all opportunities for French schools. The Free School Act in Nova Scotia (1864), and the Public School Act of Prince Edward Island also accepted only public and "neutral" schools. Acadians therefore started to fight again to redress obvious wrongs. At Caraquet the stubbornness of provincial authorities on the matter in 1871 led to riots, and the death of Louis Mailloux and John Gifford. A 1970s song and a subsequent musical by Calixte Duguay made a symbolic figure of Louis Mailloux, as a victim of an oppressive system in which Acadians were denied a place as equals. Rioting for schools was not limited to the 19th century: in the 1990s, parents would lead a major fight against the province of New Brunswick to preserve schools as major commuity resources at Saint-Simon and Saint-Sauveur.

Religious orders, meanwhile, carried on their mission of developing French instruction. On Prince Edward Island, the sisters of the order of Notre-Dame added two new convents, one at Souris in 1881 and one at Rustico in 1882. In New Brunswick the first French-speaking nuns, Les Hospitalières de Saint-Joseph, taught in the schools of Tracadie as early as 1873; the sisters of Notre-Dame at Caraquet and Saint-Louis de Kent in 1873; in 1903, Les Filles de la Sagesse arrived at Edmundston. In Nova Scotia, Father Hubert Giroir, vicar of Arichat, built two academies and in 1856 brought the sisters of Notre Dame to look after the girls, and in 1860 the Christian Brothers to look after the boys. Because of the bishop and the Tupper law of 1864, the brothers left that year, and the nuns in 1901. Les Filles de Jésus arrived at Arichat in 1902 and at Chéticamp in 1903 and have been working there ever since.

The Eudist fathers opened a college in Church Point, Nova Scotia, now Université Sainte-Anne, in 1890, and another one at Caraquet, New Brunswick in 1899 which was transferred to Bathurst in 1915 after a fire. In 1946 they opened Collège Saint-Louis in Edmundston.

Gradually, lay teachers started to replace sisters and brothers in Acadian schools. Often poorly paid and not particularly well-trained, they worked in difficult situations and faced difficulties in preparing for their role as teachers in French, as most education programs were in English only. Summer courses at Université de Moncton and the new school buildings erected since 1960 have changed the situation, and the teachers, especially in New Brunswick, are now adequately paid and well qualified. Acadians can now choose to study in French or in English, a language they usually know anyway. Many studies have proven repeatedly that being instructed in one's mother tongue yields better overall results than being caught between two languages, one at home and one at school.

Official changes in the school system that had been solidly anglophone-oriented after the 1870s were the result of long and intense lobbying by dedicated Acadian individuals and societies. In some cases those societies had education as their primary if not only goal. In 1919 the Société Saint-Thomas d'Aquin was founded on Prince Edward Island. In New Brunswick the Association Acadienne d'Education looked after the betterment of French in the schools from 1936 to 1968. In 1968 the Société Nationale des Acadiens took over, and part of its responsibilities for New Brunswick were gradually shifted to the Société des Acadiens du Nouveau-Brunswick. In Nova Scotia the Société Saint-Pierre, founded in 1948, did the same, and more recently the Fédération Acadienne de la Nouvelle-Ecosse (FANE) became active. The FÉPANE (Fédération des Parents Acadiens de la Nouvelle-Ecosse) is now the main lobbying agent for instruction in French. First on Prince Edward Island in 1894, then in

*Père Maurice LeBlanc, musician, visual artist and
former president of FANE.*

Nova Scotia from 1930, and finally in New Brunswick after 1942,
parent-teacher associations were also on the forefront in promoting
Acadian schools.

Teachers also organized. In July 1911, at the Teachers' Congress for the Maritimes, an association of French teachers, was created and summer courses were organized for them. Today each Maritime province has its teachers' associations for people teaching French as a first language. In each province Acadian teachers have slowly replaced teachers coming from other provinces or Europe to teach French as a second language.

Although simply part of a long-overdue recognition of Acadian presence, decisions made by provincial governments overwhelmingly made up of anglophones have gradually strengthened the opportunity for young Acadians to be educated in their own language. On Prince Edward Island the Evangeline region obtained a French school district in 1972; a French school was created in Charlottetown in 1980, and both could be unified under a French school board.

In Nova Scotia, although "bilingual" schools had gradually come to be tolerated in Acadian regions, Law 65 in 1981 gave Acadians the right to their own schools if they so desired and in 1990 it became obvious that French schools were needed on the model of the famed "Carrefour du Grand Havre" in Dartmouth, although the Clare-Argyle school board used French as a working language. The provincial CSAP (Conseil Scolaire Acadien Provincial), elected by all Acadians and francophones throughout the province is now a school board, and offers at last management of French schools by those who use them. A special section of the Department of Education deals with programs for Acadian schools, and a centre at Université Sainte-Anne prepares materials adapted to the Acadian reality in Nova Scotia. In New Brunswick the Department of Education has had two deputy ministers since 1964, one French and one English and the linguistic duality in its services was established in 1974.

The next step, started with the volume *Les Maritimes*, trois provinces à découvrir (Les Editions d'Acadie, 1987), is to have governments understand the need for textbooks produced by Acadian specialists for Acadian schools. Departments of education and some centres (such as Centre Provincial de Ressources Pédagogiques at Université Sainte-Anne) try to provide materials sorely needed for instruction in French in the Maritime context. Several history books, particularly by Jacques-Paul Couturier, have been produced in recent years.

Hospitalières de Saint-Joseph, an order that also created many hospitals in Acadian regions of the Maritimes, opened a boarding school in Chatham in 1869, and the Collège Maillet in Saint-Basile which became part of the Collège Saint-Louis in Edmundston in 1963 and therefore part of the Université de Moncton network. That

Université Saint-Joseph.

university, today the largest French university outside Quebec, with 6,000 students and 20,000 graduates, was formed by combining several colleges: Université Saint-Joseph in Memramcook which moved to Moncton from 1958 to 1961; Collège du Sacré-Coeur in Bathurst which closed in 1974; Collège Saint-Louis in Edmundston, and Collège Jésus-Marie at Shippagan.

The Université de Moncton completely changed the face of Acadian post-secondary education. It offers all programs in French, both arts and sciences. It is the only university in the world with a program of common law in the French language and has the main Acadian research centre, Centre d'Études Acadiennes. It has programs in business, electronics and a number of fields of direct importance for the development of Acadian society. With a staff of 700 made up of scholars of French-Canadian, Acadian, other francophone and sometimes anglophone origins, it enjoys a growing national and international reputation and played a major part in recent years in making Moncton (where Radio-Canada, l'Assomption and other Acadian institutions are also located) a modern Acadian cultural centre.

The time when the only way for young Acadians to learn in their own language was to attend parochial schools without any support

Aerial view of the Université de Moncton campus.

from public funds is now over. And the time when French textbooks had to be hidden from anglophone inspectors is also over. Although it still cannot be claimed that every child from Acadian families who wishes to study in French anywhere in the Maritimes can do so, much progress has been made in regions where Acadians are a majority or a sizable number. Where they are a relatively small minority, Acadians still face the lack of French or even immersion-oriented programs. Even where they are a sizable minority, as in Moncton, many Acadians face the problem of living in one language world at school and in other worlds on the street or with their friends.

Sometimes the quality of teaching has to be questioned. As in parochial schools, where poorly paid teachers were sometimes mediocre despite their good will and hard work, recently created Acadian schools sometimes lack teachers able to teach competently various topics in French. Sciences tended to be taught in English, because teachers learned them that way. Even Université de Moncton, a supposedly totally francophone institution, was accused at one point of having engineering and other professional and scientific subjects taught largely in English from American reference books. This led to widespread reflection on a question of interest to all francophones and all Canadians about the degree of U.S. influences on our thoughts and lives. Recycling teachers, increasing book assistance from France, Belgium and Switzerland, and betterment of programs by departments of education are all solutions to that problem, which is largely a growth difficulty and not a permanent obstacle. French schools are the only way a minority child, one living partly in an anglophone environment, is going to preserve an efficient command of his or her own language.

Youth are the strength of tomorrow. Not only do parents and schools have responsibility to help the development of young Acadians for tomorrow, but young people themselves have developed youth movements, such as Conseil Jeunesse Provincial in Nova Scotia, and requested increased involvement for young people in cultural, political and economic organizations at all levels. This is why Raymond Frenette, former premier of New Brunswick decided that the theme of the 1999 Moncton francophone summit would be youth. His successor, another Acadian, Camille Thériault, is certain to make the Francophone summit an event that will prove how much l'Acadie is now increasingly the francophone part of the whole Maritime region.

V. Politics: Sharing Power

In pre-1789 France, the middle class and the peasantry were not supposed to be involved in politics. The nobility and the king had all the power, while the bourgeoisie had all the money. The only political role for peasants was to clam up and pay taxes, or to riot when they were starved. However, Acadians had early on shown clear democratic and Republican views by electing their village representatives to deal with the French or the English, selecting them usually amongst the few seigneurs in Acadie, or the emerging middle class at Port-Royal or Les Mines.

British power had changed the political environment for Acadians from bad to worse—now they were not even allowed to say anything. The system in New Brunswick prevented Acadian men, because they were Catholic, from voting or being elected until 1830. Until the 1850s, Acadians wanted to have as little to do with the English as possible, which is easily understandable, given their history. Most Acadians were poor and struggling for survival, few had professional competence, and they were often represented by others, particularly Irish Catholics.

Some Acadian men, however, entered politics during the mid-nineteenth century. In Nova Scotia, Simon d'Entremont, elected in

1836, represented Argyle in the provincial legislature from 1836 to 1840. Frédéric A. Robichaud (1785-1863) son of the founder of Meteghan and founder himself of Corberrie, was elected the same year as a Liberal to the Nova Scotia legislature, where he also served until his defeat in Clare in 1840. Anselme-François Comeau, a former pupil of an itinerant school teacher, owner of a farm and a sawmill, and postmaster for Clare in 1835, was elected for the Reformist party in 1843, 1847 and 1851. Appointed as a judge in 1848, he became the first Acadian, in 1855, to reach the legislative council of Nova Scotia.

In New Brunswick, Armand Landry, a former teacher and a farmer with liberal views, was elected for the county of Westmoreland in 1846, and again in 1853, 1854, 1856 and from 1861 to 1870. Hostile to Confederation like most Acadians (who felt they were a group distinct from their neighbours in Quebec), he also fought the building of the railroad because he saw a danger for Acadians.

On Prince Edward Island, it was not until 1854 that Stanislas Poirier was the first Acadian elected to the provincial legislature. He became House Speaker in 1873 and signed the document that linked the province to Confederation. In 1874 he became a member of parliament and in 1895 the only Acadian senator of his time. He died in 1897. Aubin Edmond Arsenault became premier by succession in 1917. Joseph-Alphonse Bernard became the first Acadian lieutenant-governor ever appointed in the Maritimes, and other Acadians have followed in his footsteps since. Prince Edward Island usually has at least one Acadian minister, such as Jérémie-Elmer Blanchard in the 1960s or Léonce Bernard more recently.

Anglophones then were not thrilled to see Acadians in politics. Hostility was great, in New Brunswick in particular, throughout the nineteenth century. Today the existence of the Confederation of Regions party indicates that an attitude similar to that which was prevalent in Orange lodges and at the Moncton town hall when Leonard Jones was mayor will be with us for a little while longer, despite the greater openness of younger generations and the progress that has been made in mutual respect between communities. When Urbain Johnson was campaigning in 1869 in Kent County, an anglophone took a shot at him with a handgun to prevent him from getting involved in politics! After his election, he had to listen one day while an anglophone colleague claimed there were more mentally diseased Acadians than anglophones, to which Johnson replied that, as far as he knew, Acadians usually sent the mentally ill to insane asylums, while their anglophone counterparts apparently sent them to the legislature.

After Confederation, Acadian involvement in all political parties became an essential element in Maritime politics, particularly in New Brunswick, where the Acadian vote has grown the most substantially.

In Nova Scotia, master mariner Charles Boudrot from Arichat was elected to the provincial legislature as a member for Richmond County and became the first Acadian in the provincial cabinet in 1883. Ambroise H. Comeau, businessman from Clare and owner of A.H. Comeau Q.G. Ltd., was elected municipal councillor at age 24, then warden at 28, before being elected Liberal MLA for Digby in 1890. Several times a member of the provincial government, in 1907 he became the first Acadian senator from his province. Joseph-Willie Comeau, a former fishmonger and elementary school teacher who had lived in Paris for a few years, was also elected for Digby as a Liberal in 1907. He was Minister several times between 1911 and 1948, when he became a senator.

Acadians had obviously started to look for representation not only within the political parties and the legislative bodies but within government, even where they were a minority. Louis-Roland Comeau, born in 1941 and a former science student at Université de Moncton who became the head of the Nova Scotia Power Corporation, was a minister in the Conservative government in Ottawa from 1968 to 1972, representing Canada at the United Nations and on the Canada-France commissions, among other things, after which he became president of Université Sainte-Anne. He is now president of NAVCanada, a national air traffic organization.

The Nova Scotia Conservative government of 1991 had two Acadian ministers, Guy Leblanc (responsible for Acadian affairs) and Neil Leblanc. Today, the Liberal government has had Allister Surette of Argyle and Wayne Gaudet of Clare as Acadian affairs ministers, the last one having been the first Acadian legislative speaker. Russell MacLellan, son of a French mother and a former student at Poitiers, is the first Nova Scotian premier of francophone origin, and the first one to speak French. Federally, Gérald Comeau, a Conservative MP, now an Acadian senator in Ottawa, was replaced by Liberal Coline Campbell when the Mulroney government was re-elected in 1988. The Conservative provincial government of John Buchanan appointed Jean-Denis Comeau as an advisor on Acadian affairs for Nova Scotia at the turn of the 1980s: this position is now occupied by Paul Gaudet, an educator and former FANE director. Increasingly, interest in providing programs for Acadians is not a partisan issue, all the more after Acadians in Nova Scotia and elsewhere have shown that their long-held attachment to the Liberal party is not unconditional.

The Liberal party had been the party of French Canadians, the party of Wilfrid Laurier and the party of Pierre Trudeau. It was the party that had fought conscription during the two world wars, which the majority of Acadians had not wanted. However, Acadians could be found on both sides, often for reasons that had to do more with local politics and potential pork barrel rewards than with fundamental issues. The letter by Marichette on elections, published in *L'Evan-*

MARTINE JACQUOT

Jean-Denis Comeau, former Nova Scotia advisor on Acadian affairs.

géline in 1895, indicates that bottles of rum, barrels of flour, fistfights if necessary—every trick in the book was used to win an election in the Maritimes.

In New Brunswick, Auguste Renaud who had arrived in Acadie as a French sailor in 1860 and become a farmer and school teacher in Bouctouche, was elected MP for Kent County in 1867, becoming the first non-Acadian francophone to be elected to the House of Commons. Accused of patronage in favour of Acadians, he was defeated and his last years were spent in the provincial bureaucracy. Lévite Thériault, elected for Victoria-Madawaska in 1867 as a Conservative, was the first francophone to serve within the provincial cabinet, from

Guy LeBlanc, former Education Minister of Nova Scotia.

which he resigned to protest the law of 1871 that went against French public schooling. His criticism of government provoked new elections in 1874 and he was re-elected.

Sir Pierre-Armand Landry, born in 1846, son of Armand Landry, and a product of the college in Memramcook, was elected MLA for

Westmoreland in 1878 and became minister of public works from 1878 to 1882 and provincial secretary in 1913. He was accused by anglophones of being too Acadian, and accused by Acadians of being too close to the English, a reality many Acadian politicians had to face in a system where they would never be in the majority, either in a party or government. Pierre-Armand Landry was the first Acadian to serve in the cabinet of New Brunswick and on the province's supreme court, and became the only knighted Acadian in 1916, a distinction still held.

Pierre-Jean Veniot, as we mentioned, was the most influential Acadian politician of his time and the first Acadian premier of New Brunswick, paving the way for Louis Robichaud, Raymond Frenette and Camille Thériault today.

Pascal Poirier, the first Acadian from New Brunswick to be named to the Senate, was a major figure in Acadian political and cultural nationalism. Born in Shediac in 1852, he became at age 20, while still at the college in Memramcook, postmaster of the House of Commons, a job he kept until 1885. In 1895 he was named a senator by Sir John A. Macdonald, following a massive campaign by *le Moniteur Acadien*, Acadian societies and many numerous Acadians who signed petitions to have a senator in Ottawa. One of the founders of the Société Nationale des Acadiens in 1881, he served as its first president, organized some of the first Acadian conventions and presided over the Institut Canadien-Français in Ottawa. He wrote a number of books, in particular on Acadian language and history, before his death in 1933.

The election of Liberal lawyer Louis J. Robichaud, a former student of Université Laval in Quebec City, as premier of New Brunswick in 1960 was of great significance and opened a new era for Acadian rights. His government solved educational problems, such as the inequality of grants for English and Acadian schools in the province. He started programs to redress the imbalance between the province's industrialized regions and the Acadian regions, which had not had the same opportunities to develop, especially in the north of the province. Conscious of the need to maintain a professional elite, he was instrumental in creating Université de Moncton. To some extent his era was the equivalent for Acadians of the Quiet Revolution in Quebec under Jean Lesage.

After Robichaud there was no turning back. The two main communities of New Brunswick, anglophone and francophone, had to be provided equal opportunities. No premier of the province could now go back to the attitudes that had prevailed in the nineteenth century. Each government now has several Acadian ministers, and no party could survive without the Acadian vote. Acadians can become leaders of the major political parties if they are qualified and sufficiently astute. With a century of practice, Acadians have now learned how to play the game in New Brunswick.

Talking to younger Acadians when a movie about him by Acadian film maker Herménégilde Chiasson was launched in Moncton in 1989, Louis Robichaud indicated how much the public use of French had changed since the 1960s, in part because of actions taken by his government. Before in English-speaking environments Acadians spoke softly, if at all, in French. The "Speak White!" command from irate anglophones was not imaginary. Sometimes, as in the case of Bathurst, youths from differing linguistic backgrounds fought openly on the street. Some restaurants would not serve French customers. Many Acadian parents of the 1940s and 1950s believed that their children should not learn French because the sole language of money, power and business was English, an attitude that still surfaced damagingly in some Acadian regions when problems are discerned.

Parents in Acadian regions throughout Nova Scotia thought that "bilingual" schools were the ideal answer. We now know they are not. We also know that French is a language of money, business and power, just like Japanese, German and Spanish. It is a way to communicate not only in words but in cultural terms. Can culture survive without language? How much is the original language worth in preserving one's culture?

Those questions can now be debated by Acadians because they have the choice. The Robichaud government of the 1960s, the Quiet Revolution and what followed in Quebec, the revival of francophone groups throughout Canada, the coming to power of Pierre Trudeau—the new Wilfrid Laurier-and the 1968 Official Languages Act all enabled the French language to have more than a clandestine existence inside the family circle. Which French? Acadians had to be convinced that their brand of French was not "bad" French, but just one of the many varieties of French that exist. Writers, educators and linguists had to do that. Confidence and assertiveness in the public domain were results of the brilliant work done by Acadian politicians and others from the mid-nineteenth to the mid-twentieth century.

Quebec-born Jean-Maurice Simard, appointed minister several times in the Conservative governments of Richard Hatfield, was a driving force behind the provincial law that officially recognized the equality of the English and French communities in New Brunswick in 1981. Later made a senator, he was instrumental in obtaining funds to

Aldéa Landry, former vice-premier of New Brunswick.

set up an Acadian daily.

Aldéa Landry, vice-premier in the all-Liberal government elected in New Brunswick in 1988 and a former president of the provincial Liberal party, was the first Acadian woman to reach such political heights. And many federal ministers, such as Roméo LeBlanc, well-

Senator Jean-Maurice Simard.

---

known as fisheries minister during the Trudeau years, or Bernard Valcourt, also a fisheries minister under Brian Mulroney, represented Acadian interests in Ottawa. The first has become the first Acadian Governor-General, the second was the first Acadian to lead the New Brunswick Conservative party, a position now held by Bernard Lord,

Former federal minister Bernard Valcourt.

another Acadian.

In the 1970s a group of Acadians tried to create a political vehicle for Acadians, somewhat along the lines of the Parti Québécois in Quebec, called the Parti Acadien. Despite strong showings in some regions, particularly in northeastern New Brunswick, and 12 per cent of voters in 1978, it never received enough financial, institutional or electoral support to elect any candidates to office and disappeared as an official party in the early 1980s. It lacked the presence of a René Lévesque at the helm, and no leader of a major party wanted to come aboard. Most Acadian politicians seemed to feel at home within the two major parties, although ordinary Acadians continue to wonder whether a politician, once elected, will forget the needs of his Acadian constituents and support the system in place in order to be re-elected. One of the heavyweights in the Liberal government of Jean Chrétien, Doug Young, went down to defeat before an NDP candidate, Yvon Godin, because he was felt to be too far from his constituents' concerns.

In the 1980s Acadians also discovered the importance of local and municipal politics to ensure respect for their Acadian identity in the Maritime provinces.The prefect of Clare Jean Melanson, is now president of the FANE in Nova Scotia. In New Brunswick, an attempt at regrouping mayors of francophone municipalities in a common organization with specific lobbying powers has been going on for a few years, with growing success. Ex-mayor of Moncton, Léopold Belliveau, who was in power for nine years is probably the most obvious proof that Acadians now have some real presence in municipal politics.

After being excluded from the political process under both colonial regimes and for a long time afterward, Acadians have learned the importance of power. Political power enables them to fight more openly and vigorously for their rights, provides them with inside information on possible developments and makes anglophones aware of Acadian needs from within, and not simply through lobby groups. Acadian MLAs, MPs and senators, who are now members of the Association Internationale des Parlementaires de Langue Française (AIPLF), the international association of French-speaking parliamentarians, are proof that a lot of progress has been made in the field that is essential to guarantee their linguistic rights. Acadians are now considered as equal partners in New Brunswick, and in the other two Maritime provinces their special needs as minorities, are taken into account, although the defense of rights will always be a need for minority groups the world over. Row figures on linguistic transfers are often misleading. There are more bilingual people in the Maritimes today then ever, knowledge of French is improving both as a first and second language, its use in business, politics and cultural exchanges is more obvious and more important to our presence in a global economy.

VI. Women: An Essential Presence

Today, politics, like other fields of activity, is open to Acadian women. It was not always the case, although Acadian women have always been strong and, according to chronicler Marichette, were quite conscious in the 1890s that they had more brains than men even though at the time they could not vote in any of the Maritime provinces! Women obtained the right to vote federally only in 1918 and were allowed to vote by the same year in Nova Scotia, by 1919 in New Brunswick, and only by 1922 on Prince Edward Island, still almost twenty years earlier than women in Quebec. However their social importance was enormous all along. Women fought alongside the men to make the new Acadie a place where one could live, feel at home and raise families. Many are remembered as strong individuals, such as the nineteenth century character "la grande Mercure" often quoted by Régis Brun. Women were aware that nothing could be done without them—the only hope of survival for Acadians was to have children and settle new land, and women were the only ones who could give birth to those children, raise them and instil the Acadian heritage for the future.

To those for whom motherhood was not the world of their dreams, a career as a religious sister or a teacher was usually the only possibility until the 1940s. Several major characters in Canadian religious orders for women were Acadians who showed the full range of their abilities in working for others. Eléonore Thibodeau (1811-83), born in Quebec of an Acadian family, was one of the founders of Congrégation des Soeurs Grises and devoted her whole life in Bytown (later called Ottawa) to the sick and to orphans. Evangeline Gallant, from Egmont Bay, P.E.I., was from 1935 to 1936 mother superior of Soeurs Grises de la Charité in Montreal, an order dedicated to hospital work, helping the blind, and opening schools, work for which the Catholic Church and the province of Quebec recognized her enormous contribution. These women might, in other cultures and other times, have been surgeons, politicians, or explorers, but they chose avenues available to them in their day to express their capabilities.

Discovering that some of the best-known Acadian women of our century had served in religious orders before pursuing a lay career is therefore not surprising. The author Antonine Maillet is one woman who followed this path. Corinne Gallant, a philosopher and feminist who has contributed much to raising feminine consciousness in New Brunswick, left a religious community in the 1970s and continued to teach philosophy at Université de Moncton while encouraging the development of several organizations to help improve the status of women in New Brunswick. These organizations included Femmes Acadiennes de Moncton (FAM), Institut d'Education et d'Apprentissage pour les Femmes (IEAF) and the provincial advisory council on the status of women, Conseil Consultatif sur la Condition de la Femme du Nouveau Brunswick (CCCFNB). She also wrote and practised photography, co-authoring with poet Dyane Léger *Visages de Femmes* (Faces of women) in 1988. Younger women have obviously been less inclined to take part in religious orders.

One of the problems with recorded history, which tends to emphasize great deeds and events of supposedly major significance, is that for most women, making history had more to to do with successfully completing the child-rearing, daily chores and constant work that enabled society to function effectively. In the nineteenth century more Acadian clothes were made by women, who used wool or flax to make shirts, long trousers and vests for the men, and petticoats and short capes for themselves. Preparing flax or wool was an activity that required time and encouraged women to work in groups. Mechanization and changes in the structure of society have made this a thing of the past for most, but have not eradicated tight social relations in Acadian regions.

The community feeling has remained quite strong. The association Les Dames d'Acadie is still growing, as are many other associations and networks. Despite this, inequalities continue. In New Brunswick, for instance, Acadian women are sometimes still paid less for the same jobs than Acadian men and anglophone women. Despite the official policy of equality between anglophones and francophones in New Brunswick, Acadian women were a few years ago still paid $3,000 less than unilingual anglophones if they spoke English, and $1,200 less than bilingual anglophones even when they were bilingual. An Acadian woman with a university education might still earn $15,000 less than a man with the same level of education. Myths about the sexes are as hard to shake among Acadians as they are elsewhere, although progress is being made.

Acadian women in the traditional village were busy all the time. They worked at home and were also needed in the fields, leaving the children in charge of a grandmother and running back home to feed babies, prepare men's meals and all of their housework. Having little other choices throughout the nineteenth and early twentieth centuries than to be a mother, the Acadian woman cared for her children and educated them, nursed the sick, cooked, did the necessary needlework, cleaned, tended her garden and usually worked on the household items that have become "crafts" today, such as hooked rugs or quilts both of which were originally made with recycled clothes. They often traded these for items needed in the household with the *colporteurs* (peddlers) who went from village to village. Women had to

MARTINE JACQUOT

Novelist Jeannine Landry-Thériault.

assist each other in childbirth. Even if there was a doctor, often not much money was available to call him in most villages. Some midwives became famous. One of them, Dame Edith Pinet, from the Acadian peninsula, was celebrated in the movie *Une sagesse bien ordinaire* (A very real wisdom) and in a book by novelist Jeannine Landry-Thériault of Caraquet, *La Vie au bout des doigts.*

Gradually, women decided to have fewer children, without paying much attention to the fact that going against nature was a "mortal sin" in the eyes of the most conservatively minded in the Catholic Church, and they moved to other spheres of activity. Like everywhere else, modern conveniences helped. Women had had little time on their hands when they had to wash everything by hand, carry water from a brook and tend to their laundry with irons warmed on woodstoves before electric power was available. Some women spent a whole day washing their children's clothes! In traditional Acadian society, the only time women were free was during the evenings, when they would knit or quilt, and sing complaintes (laments) or tell tales for their children thus keeping the Acadian oral heritage alive.

Women were one of the pillars of Catholic life. In most parishes they were part of organizations set up to help the priest, and women educated their children in the faith and taught them to recite prayers.

The history of Acadian women is now increasingly recorded in books such as *Acadienne de Clare* by Edith Comeau-Tufts or *Nous les femmes* by Cécile Gallant. Rights acquired by anglophone women in the Maritimes are now also open to Acadian women.

On Prince Edward Island, two Acadian women were elected as mayors of Summerside in the late 1970s—Frances Perry and Anne-Marie Perry. Bas-Caraquet had the first woman mayor of an Acadian township—Roberta Dugas, who was elected in 1974 and re-elected in 1980. Caraquet elected its first woman councillor, Louise Blanchard, in the 1970s. Shippagan has had women as town councillors and Memramcook has had a woman mayor. Aldéa Landry became a powerful symbol of women's presence in New Brunswick politics, as vice-premier in a Liberal government of Frank McKenna. Ann Breault and Marcelle Mersereau were also elected to the provincial government of New Brunswick. Pierrette Ringuette-Maltais from Madawaska and Liberal Coline Campbell have served as MPs in Ottawa.

Women have also made gains in business. For example Lise Ouellette has been the coordinator of the francophone federation of farmers in northwestern New Brunswick. And in education and nursing, women are now the larger number. The challenge of the 1990s is largely economic equality.

Although conscious of their interests and rights, Acadian women may not look as radically "feminist" as their Québécois or U.S. counterparts, but many know how to demand what they want if they have to, and some have reached highly praised professional positions. Laetitia Cyr-Thériault, a native of Baie Sainte-Anne who worked as a teacher in Grand-Sault and in Woodstock before choosing a career in radio and television, became the first female director of Radio-Canada

MARTINE JACQUOT

Author Edith Comeau-Tufts in Acadian dress.

---

for the Atlantic region in 1978. Nancy Juneau has fought for francophones outside Quebec on the board of Radio-Canada. Muriel Roy, a doctor of sociology and demography, is a former director of Centre d'Etudes Acadiennes and was actively involved in finding a solution to the problem of Acadians expelled to create Kouchibouguac park in the 1970s. Mathilda Blanchard, after a career as a teacher, worker and hairdresser, became one of the best known and controversial union leaders in the Caraquet region while working inside the Conservative party: a movie is now retelling her career. Other women are lawyers, civil servants, journalists or photographers, and quite a number have made names for themselves in the arts. Without women, Acadie would not exist, and without Acadian women, the Maritimes would be poorer in many ways.

Many symbols of Acadie have been female: Marie, the Blessed Virgin (whose name was often a first name for Acadian girls); Sainte-Anne (after whom many places are named); Evangeline, a folk heroine; and characters of women who came back, such as Antonine Maillet's Pélagie, and Madeleine LeBlanc.

Maillet's *La Sagouine* has made us aware of how dreadful it was to be a poor woman in Acadie between the late 1930s and the early 1950s, and Maillet has also created those brilliant indominable characters who play tricks on the mafiosi and the police in her many novels about rum-running and liquor smuggling in the 1920s and 1930s. Jeannine Landry-Thériault has shown how difficult it was for a young woman to escape monotonous village life in the 1940s, and women memorialists such as the late Lina Madore from Madawaska (who raised fifteen children before starting to write), Berthe Cyr-Cou-lombe and many others have told us how things really were in times of poverty and economic hardship, despite the great mottos of Acadian unity. Much has been written by Acadian women in recent years, and this is just the latest indication of the role women have played since the birth of Acadie as keepers of traditions and living memories of the world around them. Major young writers like Dyane Léger, Germaine Comeau, and Gracia Couturier are proof that women have a strong voice among Acadians.

VII. A Special Region: The "Republic" of Madawaska

Acadians from Sainte-Anne-des-Pays-Bas (now Fredericton) went up the Saint John River in the 1780s after being expelled from their lands for a second time. They arrived in a region that would be claimed by both Lower Canada (Quebec) and New Brunswick and would be the subject of a border dispute between Maine and New Brunswick. It was not a poor region. Although not close to the sea like all the other Acadian regions at the time, it was a place where commercial farming was possible.

When Acadians reached the Madawaska, they met French Canadians who were already there, because Sieur de la Chenaye had received the region from the French governor at Quebec in 1683. Lower Canada was trying to maintain its authority over the territory, partly to protect transportation routes, but New Brunswick felt that the French Canadians were trespassing on land that international treaties had guaranteed to them. As Lower Canada wanted most of the territory in the Madawaska and the Restigouche, little agreement was possible. The inhabitants petitioned Governor Carleton so that the question could be solved, but by then the United States had come into the picture. The inability to agree where the border was did not assuage the fears of Madawaskayans, particularly during the War of 1812 and when Americans moved into the Madawaska region after 1817. The dispute was finally settled in 1842 with the Webster-Ashburton Treaty, which gave away a large chunk of British territory and made the Saint John River a border. The New Brunswick-Quebec boundary was finally clarified in 1885.

In 1900, of the 30,000 inhabitants in the whole of Madawaska, 14,000 lived in New Brunswick, and 16,000 in Maine. When Thomas Albert wrote *Histoire du Madawaska* (1920, republished 1982), he added the subtitle "Between Acadie, Quebec and the United States." Their ambivalent Acadian and Québécois identity, their closeness to the United States, and the distance between them and other Acadian centres in New Brunswick gave people from Madawaska a feeling that they were unique—not quite Acadians and not quite French Canadians. They are usually referred to as Brayons from the brayes they used to bray flax (the word brayes or brayons also means "clothes" in some forms of French).

Their feeling of a regional identity all their own is best expressed in the notion of the mythical "Republic of Madawaska," where Acadians are one of the ethnic groups present although definitely the main one. An old colonist is supposed to have given the answer, "I am a citizen of the Republic of Madawaska" to a French official on tour, and the symbol has stuck ever since and has been used by Madawaska representatives at the legislative assembly in Fredericton such as Dr. Lorne Violette in the 1930s.

The capital of the "Republic" is Edmundston, which was founded as the village of Petit-Sault (Little Falls) on the Saint John River in 1820. It became Edmundston in 1853 in honour of New Brunswick lieutenant-governor Sir Edmund Walker Head, who had just opened the road between Grand Sault (Grand Falls) and Petit Sault. The name "Madawaska" comes from the presence of a Malecite village named "Madoueska"—"place of the porcupines" (the word

Edmundston, New Brunswick.

madouesse was used in some regions of Acadie to designate the porcupine). The region gave itself a coat of arms in 1949, and an Order
of the Republic is presided over by ten "Knights" and the mayor of
Edmundston as president.

The coat of arms of Edmundston itself recalls the many identities
present in the "Republic"—-the Québécois, Acadians, Irish, Malecites
and Scots. The Scot, Donald Fraser, founded in 1916 the pulp and
paper firm that no visitor to Edmundston can miss, as it is located
partly in Edmundston and partly in Madawaska, Maine, where about
5,000 francophones live. Edmundston itself has more than 10,000
inhabitants, and the whole Madawaska region of New Brunswick has
about 30,000. An important agricultural region, it resembles Quebec
more than Acadie, although the Brayons are keen to mark their
differences with the Québécois.

Politicians such as Jean-Pierre Ouellet, Roland Beaulieu, or Bernard
Valcourt have come from Madawaska. Singers such as Martine Michaud,
Roch Voisine, Annick Gagnon or Etienne Deschênes also come from the
region that geographer Adrien Bérubé wanted to broaden into a northern
New Brunswick region called "Marévie" in the 1980s. Writers Serge
Patrice Thibodeau and Rino Morin-Rossignol come from Madawaska.

The college in Edmunston is now part of the campus of Université de Moncton with special programs in forestry and in computer
science. The Foire Brayonne, an economic and cultural event, is after

more than ten years, one of the largest French festivals in the Maritimes. The Salon du Livre (book fair) remains the largest in the Maritimes. On the whole, les Brayons are considered to be extroverted, talkative and dynamic people, not at all the cliché of the shy Acadian. They are, despite an obvious connection with l'Acadie, members of a community with its own distinctive identity.

VIII. Other Francophones: Ancient Memories and Recent Arrivals

Acadians share a fascinating history and a love of the land and the sea, and they all know how difficult it has been for families to survive and for communities to grow. Acadians who were gradually integrated into the anglophone population rarely did so of their own free will, but were forced to because of lack of schools, the need for work, or sometimes for more pleasant reasons—love, marriage or business interests. Most of these consider themselves "Acadians," a subgroup of the anglophone community with a different ethnic background and a few surviving traditions. The same would be true of the French Huguenot population, former arch-rivals of Acadians. Anyone named DesBarres probably would no longer speak French today, but would probably be proud of their French ancestry, sometimes using the benefit of immersion programs for their children, which can only be of service to the whole community.

Making a distinction today between Acadians and other francophones may seem difficult, and yet it is fundamental. Some French people in Halifax, Fredericton or elsewhere in the Maritimes, although close to certain acts of Acadian culture, do not feel "Acadian," if only because the regionally diverse Acadian French spoken is a specific form of the French language. Some people from Quebec are not considered Acadian by Acadians themselves and the Brayons do not consider themselves solely Acadian.

It would be easy to label any Maritime French-speaking person Acadian. Anglophones sometimes do, and yet it is not exactly correct. Many Acadians have nothing but their ethnic background to justify the claim that they are Acadian and a number of Acadians feel, as Louisiana Cajuns do, that one can be Acadian without speaking French, having had no schooling in that language (and no other choice than to learn English). Some Acadians are the result of mixed marriages (one has an American mother, one has an Irish father) which accounts for some Leblancs not speaking French, while Butlers or Kellys can be pure "Acadiens"! And many francophones have, over the course of the nineteenth and twentieth centuries, joined Acadians in their fight for francophone rights and a collective identity. Priests, journalists, politicians, writers, all have worked with the notion that Acadie is not just folklore or the memory of a people, but a reality.

Even ethnic Acadians who became anglophones have furthered the Acadian cause. Unless they ceased to proclaim their ethnic heritage, often because of the anti-French racism they might have been subjected to, they advanced the development of a multiethnic, multiracial and more open society from which discrimination on account of background or cultural traits should be absent. But their acceptance of the idea that culture and language were not related proved to be a double-edged sword. Of course, culture is far more than language alone, but it is impossible not to see that anglicization turns Acadians, after a few generations, into members of the North American English society for which "Acadian" comes to mean essentially folklore and history. Even though individual ethnic pride is important to a person, no modern day "Acadie" could be based on those elements alone as a collective project by a francophone community.

For Acadians who want to retain their identity, the question is not simply one of retaining language, but of learning the new culture that is carried by the French language while retaining the deep family and community roots that are present in the Acadian language and which would be lost forever if all Acadians were to speak only English or nothing but a sanitized "international" type of French. Acadians who want to retain their French language, however, still face discrimination and hostility, if not outright instances of racism. They may not have to change their name from Leblanc to White, but they may not be judged totally "equal" to some people of English-Canadian origin. The presence among them of a number of francophones from other places, the growing international value of Acadian institutions such as Université de Moncton and the growing fame of Acadian writers give means to convince adversaries that a francophone presence in the Maritimes is a major asset at a time when international competition is fierce. French-only schools are an important tool in maintaining an Acadian-French community that can also participate fully in the cultural life of anglophone North America.

The link between Maritime francophones and the teaching of French language and literature in primarily anglophone Maritime universities is part of the reality of the region. The presence of a Quebec delegation in Moncton which develops formal ties with the government, universities and business community of the only French-speaking province in Canada, is also an important part of the network of support for the Acadian community.

How many non-Acadian francophones live in the Maritimes today? The numbers are relatively small: about 500 French from France, a few people of Swiss-French origin, several hundred Québécois and other French Canadians, a few Belgians, a few Haitians and some people from other countries that are at least partly francophone, such as Algeria, Tunisia, Lebanon, or Vietnam. On the whole, non-Acadian francophones number around 5,000 at the most and may usually be found living in major cities such as Halifax or Moncton. The Fédération Acadienne de la Nouvelle-Ecosse estimates that half the francophone community in Halifax, which also enjoys the presence of an "Alliance Française" association, is of French Canadian or French origin, with the remainder being Acadian. Some came to study and stayed, in increasing numbers (albeit still small) since Canada (and not only Quebec) is now the land of choice for people from France who want to emigrate. Some came through marriage or family ties, such as the young French girl living in Cape Breton played by French actress Miou-Miou in Robert Frank's movie *Candy Mountain*. Some came as cooperants (French national civil service) for Acadian institutions and stayed. Some, such as the French Canadian members of the military stationed at Greenwood or Halifax, even when here for a few years only, may continue to keep alive important ties with the Maritimes; more and more choose to remain here after leaving the Forces.

It is impossible to live in French in the Maritimes and ignore the Acadian reality as the basis of francophone life. Some recent immigrants share common goals with Acadians and have chosen to work within Acadian society, while others feel more part of an international francophone community than of a regional one. The presence of all, however, is a major asset when it comes to the need for organizations, institutions, schools, film societies, and other structures for a community connected by its use of one of the two official languages of Canada.

Anyone who has attended a successful presentation of *La Sagouine* in Halifax, a city originally built to promote British and Protestant identity in what was Acadie, knows that a vibrant francophone community is possible even in a minority setting. Moncton is offering more and more international ties in all fields, not only with France and Quebec, but with African countries and the francophone community in Belgium.

Often, new francophone immigrants bring with them a level of expertise that would be helpful to any community. This is true in the case, for instance, of Haitian writer and professor Gérard Etienne in Moncton; late Swiss chef Alex Clavel, who brought to the Maritimes new standards in his field; director Normand Godin (originally from Quebec), sculptor Claude Chaloux (from Quebec) or singer/songwriter Patrice Boulianne (from Manitoba) in Nova Scotia's Baie Sainte-Marie region; writer Charles Baurin, who came from Belgium to live and teach in Halifax; Christiane Saint-Pierre, a novelist from Quebec, now living in Shippagan, who represented Acadian writers on the New Brunswick arts council; artist Edith Bourget, actively involved in the arts scene in Edmundston, N.B.; manager and developer Gaston Chagnon in Halifax, who is originally from Quebec and has supported Acadian organizations for decades; cultural journalists and writers like Martine Jacquot (originally from France) in Nova Scotia or David Lonergan (originally from the Gaspé) in New Brunswick.

What may be missing for Acadian regions is a consistent immigration policy, along the lines of the one for Quebec, that would ensure that the French-speaking value of these regions is enhanced, if only for purposes of culture, tourism and global trade. Such a program exists in Manitoba, for the benefit of the whole community. With a declining birth rate everywhere in the Western world, francophones and anglophones alike need to rely increasingly on immigration policies suited to their needs to maintain the rate of development necessary to sustain their communities. In Acadian regions, particularly, which are usually far from major service centres, the immigration question is an open one.

Some Acadians may tell you that all French people from France are like Bertrand in *Constellations* by Janice Kulyk Keefer, a Maritime English novelist: "A Français de France," as we say here: "someone whose language, looks and general skyscraping superiority are like a flaming sword brandished from a transatlantic paradise…a luckless rocket launched from the City of Light, and fallen to the brute backwoods of Acadie." Do not trust them. Of course, it is hard to consider as totally "equal" in historic, economic and political size and importance 58 million French, more than five million Québécois, and a few hundred thousand Acadians, however "international" the Acadian network may be.

The French from France may sometimes consider themselves superior, like the type known as *maudit Français* (goddamn Frenchman) in Quebec during the 1960s. It may be harder for some francophones from Europe, where intensive schooling in French, urban culture and broad interests are a basic part of life, to work at exactly the same level as Acadians who may have had inadequate schooling in French, have come from a rural culture and possesses a limited knowledge of the outside world. Again, both have to respect the positive sides in the other's experiences. Acadians may not have read as many books, but they may know tidal winds better. Modern Acadian culture is growingly recognized the world over for its unique original flavour.

The notion of cooperation, the policy by which France sent young people to work in Acadian organizations instead of sending them off to military duties was based on that complementary approach. Cooperants working for Acadian newspapers brought knowledge of journalism or new design ideas and took back to France, or other parts of the world, after two years, a better knowledge of the Maritimes and a desire to promote trade or cultural ties between this region and the places they have discovered.

Francophones who come to the Maritimes to stay permanently, are, after all, following the path of Acadians of old. Most Acadians themselves were originally peasants, labourers, and lower middle-class professionals from Poitou, Touraine, Vendée, or Limousin in central western France who were somehow convinced to come and settle in a new world. When Charles de La Tour had sought hired French workers to bring them to Acadie in 1642, many had come by waterway from regions far away in the south, north, and east of France, and even from areas outside of France such as Switzerland. The difference between Acadians and other francophones may simply be that some took the boat earlier than others who now take the plane.

Without the original Acadians, francophone life in the Maritimes today would have no strong tradition to relate to. But the stories of other francophones in the Maritimes are also rich. Even though Halifax was largely an anglophone city, it has had many ties with France over the centuries, not even considering the unfortunate fact that the Halifax explosion during the First World War was caused by the ignition of *Le Mont-Blanc*, a French ship. Halifax was, until planes systematically replaced boats for passenger traffic between Europe and North America, the main door not only to Canada but to North America, and many a French traveller went by.

Bénigne Charles Febret de Saint-Mesmin, for example, was a French émigré, one of the aristocrats who fled abroad during the French Revolution. He was on his way to Canada and went through Halifax at the end of 1793, leaving us with his impressions of the city and also of Edward Augustus, Duke of Kent, a man who spoke perfect French, as was customary at the time when it was the international language of diplomacy. Edward Augustus (Queen Victoria's father) is the member of the British royal family who, sent to the Maritimes as an administrator between 1794 and 1799, shocked the rather conservative Haligonian society with his public relationship with a French lady known as Madame de Saint-Laurent, for whom he built a lodge next to Bedford Basin, where a little belvedere can still be found. Thérèse-Bernardine Mongenet, her real name, was a brilliant lady, well-read in French and English, and her relationship with the prince is the basis of one of the great love stories of the world. Around the end of their stay in Halifax they had the pleasure to greet, among other visitors, the Duc d'Orléans, the future King Louis XVIII of France, and his brothers, one of whom became king after the fall of Napoléon I.

One of the most amazing love stories in the history of nineteenth century French literature, which was made into a movie shot in Halifax, by film maker François Truffaut, is that of Adèle Hugo, daughter of the French writer and politician Victor Hugo, and an obscure British officer, Albert Pinson. In 1863, a young woman poorly dressed for the Maritime climate arrived in Halifax, registering herself at a hotel under the name of "Miss Lewly." She stayed three years in the city, claiming to have married the man of her dreams (who actually paid little attention to her), and although she left for the Caribbean, became mentally disturbed and never married Albert, her story became a local legend after she was identified for whom she really was. It is interesting to note that she was recognized not by her English landlady, but by a Frenchman living in Halifax who was practising the art of French cuisine for a British general.

Visitors keep ties alive and often leave records of their passage for future generations, but they do not, as a rule, dig in and try to settle the land. Some French people, however, attempted that at the turn of the twentieth century. A number of French bourgeois families, often opposed to the increasingly socialist and anti-clerical learnings of France, tried to settle in various places in Canada, then largely more conservative: examples abound in Quebec, in Manitoba, and in Nova Scotia. The story of La Nouvelle France, a village founded in southwestern Nova Scotia by the Stehelin family, although it did not lead to a permanent colonization, is a real saga. In 1890, Father Blanche, the superior of the Eudists, left for Nova Scotia to found Collège Sainte-Anne, which later became Université Sainte-Anne. He took with him a young man, Jean Stehelin, who was later joined by his brothers and parents. His father, Emile, a French businessman, decided to build a lumber empire at Baie Sainte-Marie. The village

Nouvelle France, which looked like a fairytale to many Acadians, with its own electric generating system, has now disappeared, but it is part of the Acadian lore of the region as much as l'Université Sainte-Anne itself.

Acadians loved to work for "le grand Français de France" who was opening a sawmill, houses, a chapel, offices, a bakery—a whole "electric city" was created on the huge estate. The organized exploitation of the forest enabled Stehelin to ship lumber to South America, after building a train to Weymouth. This was a time when, from Bouctouche to Chéticamp, enterprising priests encouraged new business ventures to enable Acadians to remain in their parishes rather than chose exile again. Scores of distinguished visitors came by, but things did not last.

Mrs. Stehelin died, and her funeral was presided over by Monsignor Edouard LeBlanc, the first Acadian bishop. In 1912, Stehelin left La Nouvelle France and his sons carried on but were all called to war in 1914. One organized the 175th Acadian Regiment, the first group of Acadians to go and fight for France. After the father died, only Major Stehelin, the eldest son, remained at Church Point. An annual pilgrimage is made by people from the Baie Sainte-Marie to remember what could have been a major industrial centre, in French, on Acadian soil. The story is chronicled in *Electric City*, a book by Paul Stehelin, grandson of Emile and in *Loin de France*, an attempt by Germaine Comeau at recreating it for teenagers.

Other Frenchmen of the early nineteenth century had also shown an indomitable spirit of adventure and had tried to develop new projects in the Maritimes. As early as 1815 a group of Trappist monks led by Father Vincent came to Nova Scotia to find a place for a religious community. After a few years, Father Vincent founded his community in Tracadie, in the Acadian region of Pomquet in Nova Scotia in 1821 and called it Le Petit Clairvaux.

This monastery was another dream that gradually crumbled, like so many French dreams in North America. But the presence of a dedicated group of monks helped the Mi'kmaq, Acadians and many others for more than a century. Father Vincent was actively involved in fighting cholera in Halifax in 1834. He was a man with extensive medical knowledge, an interest in agriculture and a real love for the Mi'kmaq. He worked tirelessly until his death in 1853 to preserve the precarious existence of his monastery, at a time when all bishops in the Maritimes were Irish or Scottish, and when there were few missionaries for the Catholic Acadians, and very few Acadian priests, if any.

In 1857 a Belgian priest, Father Jacques, came to Tracadie and saved the monastery for another fifty years. In 1903 the Belgian community left for Rhode Island, but a group of French monks landed in Halifax under Father Villeneuve and went to Tracadie. This was not enough to save the community, which had to close in 1919. Some of its buildings are used today by a few other monks, but what remains of this French religious community is largely found in memories and on graveyard crosses. Acadian writer Ephrem Boudreau has recreated the whole story in *Le Petit Clairvaux* (1980).

Many stories of French, Québécois or other francophone visitors to the Maritimes remain to be written. Many left books and articles behind them: Prince Roland Bonaparte in 1893; journalists who wrote about Acadians; linguists such as Geneviève Massignon in the 1940s, who wrote *Les Parlers Français d'Acadie* (the first serious study of Acadian speech); ambassadors of French culture such as Philippe Rossillon in the 1970s, a man whom Prime Minister Trudeau suspected of being a French secret agent who was honored by the SNA and the Université de Moncton in 1995; moviemakers such as Québécois Pierre Perrault with *L'Acadie, l'Acadie*; writers such as Nobel Prize winner Saint-John Perse in the 1950s. Georges Nestler Tricoche acted as a correspondent for *la Revue Mondiale* in Paris in the 1920s and also published several books on the Maritimes and Newfoundland, some in French, such as *Au Maine et au Nouveau-Brunswick* (1925) or *Terre-Neuve et alentours*, and some in English.

The French Canadian Lionel Groulx, famous defender of the idea of a French Catholic state in Quebec in the 1930s, and a major historian of Canada, has left in his memoirs impressions from a visit made to Acadian regions in 1915. Grand Pré inspired him to write a novel called *Au Cap Blomidon*, in which Acadians return to their old lands, and in Moncton and other places he perceived how different Acadians, young and old, felt from their French Canadian visitors— the way they spoke, their fear of being dominated by Québécois in joint organizations, their different collective experience, all made it difficult for them to consider themselves "French Canadian" in a Québécois sense. Francophones interested in l'Acadie have done much to help rediscover the Acadian past. New ties are also established, especially in the age of the world wide web.

The rediscovery of Marichette, an ancestor of La Sagouine, was made by French professor Pierre Gérin, who had married an Acadian. The driving force behind a number of Acadian films for many years has been a man born in France, Eric Michel, a former TV journalist who contributed to the development of Radio-Canada in Moncton. Diane Poitras, a young film maker from Quebec, is now actively looking for a new flux of talent among young Acadians as head of the Moncton ONF (French NFB) documentary program. Martine Jacquot is writing a novel set in nineteenth century Acadie, recreating women's lives at the time of the age of sail. Students and professors at Université de Moncton come from French Africa, not counting constant streams of visitors from other francophone countries. Yves Beauchesne created a centre for children's literature at Université Sainte-Anne, where Norman Godin (both originally from Quebec) created among other plays his Evangeline musical drama.

The first feature film directed by an Acadian, *Le Secret de Jérôme* had Québécois as well as Acadian actors, and was shot in New Brunswick's Village Historique Acadien; *Les Portes Tournantes*, from Jacques Savoie's novel of the same title, was shot by a Quebec filmmaker with French and Québécois actors. When *Le Tapis de Grand Pré*, the film for children, was shot in Chéticamp three soundtracks were made—in standard French, in Acadian French, and in English. Acadian communities cannot live in isolation from the world, nor can the rest of the francophone world ignore them.

Some organizations created for francophones in general such as L'Alliance Française (still active in Halifax, where it was created in 1903, yet extinct in Moncton) have gradually moved towards greater Acadian participation and collaboration with Acadian organizations.

The acceptance of francophones from other countries or other parts of Canada into the fold of Acadian culture is proof that parochialism, *l'esprit de clocher*, though always present to some degree as a natural defence in any community, is not as stifling as it might have been decades ago. Acadian culture is now mature enough to accept individual influences without feeling threatened by them; on the contrary, such influences may enable diverging voices in the communities to emerge, fostering dynamic development. Today, Acadie is more interesting than ever to the world's francophone community, and such interest goes both ways. As poet Aimé Césaire, of the French Antilles, declared, the importance of a community to the world does not depend on sheer numbers, and smaller communities are as essential as larger ones, although they face many more problems in securing their future.

IX.   Acadians Outside the Maritimes

If Acadie had developed naturally, without tragic interruption, several million Acadians would probably be living in the Maritimes. After the Expulsion many Acadians settled in Quebec. Bona Arsenault, who published the most complete genealogical research on Acadians, was a Québécois politician and historian born of Acadian parents. Québécois with Acadian ancestors somewhere in their family tree are numerous today, particularly in Montreal, the Eastern Townships, and the Gaspé. Some Québécois of Acadian origin, like Hockey Hall of Fame great Jean Beliveau, or major Hollywood actress Geneviève Bujold, are extremely proud of their Acadian origin. Many expatriate Acadians will, in Canada or in the United States, meet through Acadian groups like the RAM (Rassemblement des Acadiens de Montréal). The 1994 Congrès Mondial Acadien was originally a project by André Boudreau, an Acadian living in Alberta, who felt that all branches of Acadian families should come together for the first time since the Expulsion.

Numerous other people have Acadian ancestors. Novelist Gabrielle Roy, minister Sheila Copps, singer Raoul Duguay are only a few of the millions who owe their lives to an Acadian descent, which they recognize more and more with real pride. Pop singer Madonna is linked with the Acadian family Orillon.

Over the years, a number of Acadians have also gone to work in Quebec. Writers Antonine Maillet, Jacques Savoie, Claude LeBouthillier, and Michel Roy, to name but a few, live in Montreal. Young people of Acadian descent live in Quebec, in Masssachusetts, or out west, driven there by a need for jobs. Some have left the Maritimes to find more inter-esting work, but some have left because their career could only develop elsewhere because the Maritime market was too small. The latter is particularly the case for musicians, singers or people in the performing arts, for example, the most famous Acadian actress Viola Léger, Ronald Bourgeois from Chéticamp, Edith Butler from Paquet-ville, Angèle Arsenault from Prince Edward Island, Marie-Jo Thério from Moncton, and Roch Voisine from Madawaska. Some have since come back, although an artistic or business career necessarily calls for a period in a larger francophone community than the Maritimes.

X.   A Southern Culture from Acadian Stock: The Cajuns

The existence of the Cajun community in Louisiana has been well-known to all since the seventeenth century. The first explorers, like Cavelier de la Salle, discoverered Louisiana soon after the settlement of Nova Scotia. Louisiana has had a long history of connections to France. From Cavelier de la Salle in 1682 and le Moyne d'Iberville in 1699, France had taken real interest in developing the economy of its major colony in southern North America. By 1762, Louisiana had become Spanish in large part. The many Acadians welcomed by the Spanish government at the end of the eighteenth century gave birth to a new type of Acadian population, the "Cajuns," who now number more than one million.

French travellers to Louisiana in the nineteenth century described the Cajuns as simple folk surviving in Bayou country as farmers, fisherman and trappers. Cajun women married young and had large families. Although Cajuns make up no more than one-tenth of the population of Louisiana, the descendants of settler Broussard now number more then 3,800, and the descendants of settler Mouton more than 42,000! Many stories and customs from old Acadian folklore were kept alive and adapted to a new environment. The way to get rid of a Cajun werewolf, for instance, is to throw frogs at it! The Thibaudeaus, Héberts and Martins loved to dance, spending nights in rigadoons or quadrilles, and eating gumbo. And the flavour of Cajun cooking is today known around the world, as is the hospitality of people in Acadiana, the southern Louisiana region which constitutes "L'Acadie du Sud."

These Acadians of the south developed a unique culture. Acadians of the prairies in southwestern Louisiana and Texas became cattle ranchers, and the horse became an essential part of the culture, whether to court a *jolie blonde* in the nineteenth century or to ride during Mardi Gras celebrations in Mamou. Despite some basic similarities with Acadian culture, Cajun culture has taken a different flavour in the bayous and the warm climate of the flats around Lafayette. Cajun culture survived in relative isolation until the 1950s, when the development of the oil industry started to threaten its collective survival. In recent years, pride in the Cajun heritage has grown, even though many Cajuns, in the American context, have been forced to lose their attachment to the French language, which was not taught for a long time, and strongly discouraged by the schooling system. Many Cajuns even today have no clear idea what being of Acadian descent means, because Acadian history was not taught or was camouflaged in schools.

What most people know about Cajun country is the music they have heard. In no other part of Acadie has music played such an essential role in keeping the language alive, although sometimes in limited form (verbs have only one tense in Cajun French, for instance). Cajuns, like Maritime Acadians, use language from the sea more often than is common in standard French. To turn is *virer de bord*, to tie a horse is *amarrer un cheval*, a well-dressed girl is *ben gréée*, like a schooner. If Acadians from the Maritimes have no problems eating *une galette* for Fête des Rois (Epiphany), Cajun women might feel offended by a reference to them that used the same word!

Cajuns should not be confused with Créoles, the Louisiana French aristocracy. Although their memory still haunts French films and novels, Créoles were largely wiped out after the failure of the southern Confederacy they had supported. Deeply attached to their country, most Cajuns had also, of course, been soldiers in the Confederate States Army, but very few had been officers, except for CSA general Alfred Mouton, the "Cajun general," the son of a Louisiana governor of the same family. The ruin of the Old South took with it the bilingual status of the state, leaving New Orleans a beautiful shell empty of French except for history—the famed "French Quarter" of today, with its elegant architecture. The bulk of Créole literature is now part of the French heritage of Louisiana. Cajuns remained, not only in Louisiana but in neighbouring states such as Texas, and even brought into Cajun culture people from different ethnic origins (Germans, Blacks, and Spaniards).

Names of Cajun musicians such as Ambroise Thibodeaux, Michael Doucette named Beausoleil (born in 1951), the Jambalaya Cajun Band, and singer and poet Zachary Richard (born in 1950) are now part of French musical lore the world over. Zachary Richard, whose "Réveil" was one of the highlights of the 1994 show for the Congrès Mondial in Shédiac, is as well-known in France and Italy as he is in Quebec and Acadie. A singer like Bruce Daigrepont is frequently heard in the Maritimes with a blend of rock and Cajun music. French musicians in France pick up Louisiana songs, and the "Acadie of the South" adds to the Acadian magic an exotic southern attraction. Many dream of going to a *fais-dodo* (all-night dancing party) while listening to accordion and fiddle music and the whining sound of Cajun voices that seems to convey the distress of former exiles discovering the bayous and dancing in pleasure far from the cold Maritime winters: more and more "Mardi Gras" celebrations take place in small Maritime communities.

The rebirth of an official status for the French language started in the 1960s under the influence of politicians who understood the advantages of banking on a francophone community in the state, if not redeeming the wrongs from the past, such as James Domengeaux, founder of the Codofil, which works for instruction in French and for better cultural and economic relations with francophone countries. It is currently presided over by Warren Perrin and directed by David Chéramie. Some artists and university people, such as Barry Ancelet, a folklorist who has travelled extensively to France and Canada and is defending Cajun values against total Americanization, or Zachary Richard, who chairs "Action Cadienne," have raised their profile. The defence of a separate linguistic identity in the United States is no easy task: the main Louisiana parish, Vermilion parish, has as yet no French immersion schools, although it is hoped that some will be there for the 1999 Congrès Mondial.

Cajuns are very much Acadians in many ways: ways of speaking Acadian French, attachment to tradition and Catholic values, a zest for life as an adventure to be enjoyed, a love for parties and music. They are, however, more colourful than their northern cousins: the museum in Saint-Martinville shows carnival costumes glittering to an extent rearely seen north, sometimes proudly displayed in parades and Mardi Gras festivals; their music is livelier, less prone to nostalgia; their food is a lot spicier, from the roux and gumbos to the jambalayas—lots of exotic names from the "Bayou country" those refugees from Nova Scotia settled in the eighteenth century.

Cultural, family and economic exchanges have increased in recent years between Louisiana and the Maritimes. Individuals such as René Babineau of Richibouctou who spend as much time in the southern Acadie as in the northern one, have helped to bring Cajun theatre troupes and individuals to the Maritimes. Their ability to defend French (with a blend of Acadian and standard French) is limited compared to their northern cousins: there are no French publishers in Louisiana, only a few immersion programs, and the francophone faculty of the University of Southwestern Louisiana, the "Cajun" university is by and large limited to its department of French and parts of research centres. Monsignor Nil Thériault of Baie Saint-Marie has organized travels to Louisiana for Nova Scotia Acadians who wanted to meet distant relatives, and the twinning of villages and parishes has become increasingly common.

There are now exchanges at a more official level: Nova Scotia is now in its fourth Acadian trade mission to Lafayette (for trading anything, from apples to cultural products); Les Editions d'Acadie publish Cajun writers; teachers from the Maritimes teach in Louisiana schools. Genealogy brings a fair number of Acadians together, the former exiles looking for their roots around Grand Pré and Port Royal, sometimes through organized tours (hence boosting Maritime tourism), individuals like William Gerior (Girouard) from Halifax bringing all Giroir cousins together for family gatherings: at the 1994 Congrès Mondial, family gatherings were a major feature, and it will be even more the case at the 1999 Congrès in Abbéville, La., and the whole of Acadiana.

Moncton writer Melvin Gallant wants to include, in a novel in progress about Evangeline, a trip to modern Cajunland. Such a trip will be undertaken by many in August 1999, for the second Congrès Mondial (the third being already planned, possibly, for Nova Scotia in 2004). Louisiana—and Acadiana in particular—is already seeing many visitors from France, Quebec, Acadie, like in the gathering for the Giant Omelet Festival in Abbéville. Through such personal exchanges with institutional support are new areas of francophone reality being developed. Acadians from the Maritimes play no small part in sup-porting and assisting Cajuns in such a promotion of their common identity, which is necessarily based on individual pride in being part of la francophonie first of all.

Although their cultures evolved in different ways, these two Acadies have a lot in common, not forgetting the difficulties created for them by members of their respective majorities in the past, as was documented in the 1988 Cajun movie *Belizaire le Cajun*, which was shown on cable television in the Maritimes. Glen Pitre, the director, is with Pat Mire one of the Cajun filmmakers who deal with their own reality in a state famous for movies done by filmmakers from all over the world, including a number of Quebec filmmakers. Today the international Acadian community brings support to a Cajun com-munity that is, linguistically and culturally, more in need of support than others. The fact that such a feeling of community exists at an international level, including Acadians from Canada, several Ameri-can states, France and other parts of the world is a source of pride among Acadians, who have in the past been despised and isolated.

Some Maritime Acadians left for Louisiana during the second half of the nineteenth century, feeling that better opportunities awaited them there. They were part of a larger group of Acadians who left the Maritimes, especially to find work in New England mills and fac-tories. A good number stayed and became Americans. A glance at the phone book in Saugus, a Boston suburb, tells part of the story. Most Acadian families have members in the United States. Some left more recently to further their careers. Paul Leblanc from Dieppe, a hair-dresser, received an Academy Award for his work on the movie *Amadeus*. The letters published in *L'Evangéline*, signed Marichette, tell about young Acadian girls of the 1890s who went to the States to find a "feller" and thus dressed less conservatively than in their villages, and these letters leave little doubt as to the popularity of such a move.

Many Acadians have to leave even today to pursue career goals elsewhere. Such a phenomenon is unfortunately known to all linguistic minorities who do not have control over their own political agenda and economic development. It is also the tragedy of small communities, where the elite inevitably perpetuates the privileges of a few and a certain ideology, forcing the young and the imaginative to look for a community more responsive to their talents. Even though Acadians scattered throughout the world (even to the Falklands!) in a diaspora—like that of the Jews, Blacks, or Poles, they all keep deep in themselves a part of their Acadian identity.

CHAPTER 4

Contributions to the Maritimes and Canada

I.   Culture

What defines culture? It can be, first of all, the land that surrounds us and the way it has been called, shaped by our ancestors and handed down to us. Then it is the languages we speak and the way they interrelate. Language naturally gives birth to what most of us call culture—music, literature, theatre, film, visual arts, elaborate ways to express what we feel as individuals and how we view our collective identity. But these facets of culture may reach only some of us. For all of us, however, culture also includes the way we handle ourselves in daily life, our cooking and crafts, the ways science shapes our lives, our electronic environment, and our relationship to the world through the communities we live in.

Acadian culture necessarily draws from all the elements that have influenced it, from its connections with France, its North American environment, the Canadian system and its need to preserve basic elements of life in a maritime setting. It would be absurd to think, though, that Acadian culture can be limited to what was borrowed from other cultures. On the contrary, it has produced a unique blend that can vary considerably depending on the history, work, linguistic traits and traditions of the regions we consider.

Do you think *le pâté à la râpure* (rappie pie) is an Acadian specialty? You are right if you are in southwestern Nova Scotia. But do not try to find any in southeastern New Brunswick! There what you will hear, based on potatoes and meat or clams is *une poutine râpée*, not to be confused with what the Québécois call *une poutine* (a mix of melted cheese and fries) or with what some French from France call *une poutine* (a kiss) in their region! Do not expect oysters in Baie Sainte-Marie, but savour them among P.E.I. Acadians in Malpeque! And if for some reason an Acadian from one region tells you that a clam is, in French, definitely of the masculine gender (*un coque*), while you have heard someone from another region swear it was feminine (*une coque*, as in the village name Grosses Coques), do not fret. You have just discovered that, although a nation in several pieces, Acadie—like all countries—has several regions that are in some ways quite different from one another.

II. Place Names

In the Maritimes one cannot ignore the reality of Acadian history even in regions where Acadians have now ceased to reside as a majority group, or where names have since become anglicized. Acadians have named the land and explored and defined it.

A good number of place names have changed since Acadie was French in the eighteenth century. Many names, however, have retained a connection with the original French or with a name originally borrowed by the French from an Indian word. La Hève, which became LaHave in English, came with the French from France, recalling Le Havre in Normandy, the word *havre* still being used by Acadians for a harbour. In the Annapolis Valley, which contains the highest number of old Acadian archaeological sites, Le Bassin-des-Mines became Minas Basin. La Grand Prée remained Grand Pré, even though today's village does not correspond to the original Acadian settlements, which were much larger. La Rivière-aux-Canards in the Canning area became Canard River. Pisiquid and Sainte-Famille became Windsor and Falmouth.

Even in Acadian regions, an anglicized name has often been superimposed upon the old place name, even though the old one is still used by the population. For instance, in southwestern Nova Scotia, the village of La Butte (the hill) became Meteghan River; La Rivière aux Saumons became Salmon River; Paradis Terrestre became Paradise; and Pointe-de-l'Eglise is now Church Point. Chipoudie became Shepody. Chimougoui became Chemogue, and the place in New Brunswick called Le Chemin Frigault became Frigault Road. Gradually, French names have become official again.

Towns dominated by a small anglophone elite, have names that clearly indicate their English origins—Bathurst, Newcastle and Yarmouth for instance. Sometimes the French name was nearly forgotten, as in Moncton, where until recently few people remembered

The photo above shows the remnants of a wooden aboiteau on the shores of the Minas Basin. At right are the remnants of the square-cut sod used to fill an aboiteau near Grand Pré.

that the place was called Le Coude (the bend in the river) before any English-speaking settlers settled there. Bay of Fundy was Baie Française in the eighteenth century. Sometime pronunciations are outright oddities as in "Bear River" which comes from Rivière Hébert. When francophones left in the eighteenth century, names were kept but were pronounced in a different way by the new English-speaking settlers-near Louisbourg Main À Dieu, perfectly meaningful in French (God's hand) is now called "Manadoo," a meaningless term. Tintamarre became in English Tantramar. Tintamarre means something in French (a riotous, noisy feast, still celebrated in many Acadian villages), but Tantramar has no literal meaning in English.

It has become increasingly important for Acadians to enjoy a right to the real name of the places where they live, in their own language and its original form. Most visitors will notice efforts made in this direction in recent years. But it is also important to keep alive those French-Acadian names that were given centuries ago to places we have come to love and cherish. They are an important part of our collective history and a distinctive feature of our land for tourists coming in larger numbers and contributing greatly to Maritime economies.

Some places drastically changed names, retaining perhaps a trace of their past. Beaubassin became Amherst, Cap Baptiste turned into Cape Blomidon, but Cape Sable was retained in Cape Sable; Cap-

Celebrating Tintamarre in Caraquet.

Fourchu became Yarmouth, but the name remains in Cape Forchu; Cap Fendu was translated literally as Cape Split. Chibouctou, a place never really settled by the French, became Halifax, but the French-Indian name remains in Chebucto. Some names disappeared altogether, but may surface in brands or store names to engage the tourist: the name Cobequid can be found around Truro, just as Pisiquid around Windsor. Most people today know Gaspereau more as a fish than as a place. The French presence in Charlottetown keeps alive the original name of Port Lajoie, just as the Sainte-Anne cultural centre in Fredericton reminds us that there was a French presence in the area. And what should we say about Evangeline, who, as Angèle Arsenault sings in "Evangeline, Acadian Queen," has given her name to shoe stores, mobile homes, the Land of Evangeline, Evangeline bus lines. Soon, she may be rivalled only by Champlain, whose name appears on one of the largest shopping malls in Moncton.

III. Language

One can always find Acadian friends who claim that they speak like Rabelais, Molière, or Ronsard, meaning that they are the only group to still speak the "pure" French of the seventeenth century or before, a language much more powerful, colourful and expressive than the bland "standard" French being taught in schools the world over. Credit them with possessing a basic pride, the same one Pascal Poirier expressed when he wrote his *Glossaire Acadien* in the 1930s; they are proud of their language and this, for a minority, is important. After all, Acadians have been told too often by the English, the Québécois and the French that they spoke "bad" French, a stupid reaction on the part of larger groups that themselves have many kinds of colloquial French.

Acadian French is a particular form of French. Is it rich enough to express what needs to be said? Is it complex enough to communicate more than the basic necessities of life? Is it expressive enough to convey feelings that Acadians need to communicate to themselves or others? Is it purely oral or can it be written down? What should be taught in Acadian schools now that most of them are "French" schools? These are the real questions. Neither excessive pride nor unenlightened racism are proper attitudes when it comes to useful discussions about language, which remains the basis of all cultures, regardless of continent.

Do not blindly trust anglicized Acadians who claim to be more Acadian because they have "the culture without the language." Once French is gone from an Acadian community, family or individual, it is gone for good: efforts made in the field of "immersion" programs as "refrancisation" in recent years may be useful, but have meaning only when French is still the living language of a number of people in that area. French schools with Acadian-based programs, preparing new generations for the future, were one of the important elements of development Acadians had to have to live as a full-fledged Maritime community.

The importance of a French reality in the Maritimes cannot be stressed too much as a major enrichment for all of us. Respecting Acadians' rights to their language as a fundamental part of their collective identity shows basic tolerance of others. Not respecting that principle leads to intolerance, not only towards Acadians, but towards all other groups. It also leads, as many of us are sadly aware, to dissolving Canada into a vague notion of American continental identity, which can only mean an outright flattening of our small regions' unique attributes under the massive steamroller of American power, money and unabashed self-esteem—although regionalism and linguistic diversity are more obvious in the United States today than in the 1950s.

Do Acadians still speak the way their ancestors did when they arrived from France in the seventeenth century? Of course not. Any language changes, evolves, and becomes different in every region and with every generation. The French language, which the Académie Française has imposed written standards upon since the seventeenth century, is a codified form of the language originally spoken around Paris, in the Ile-de-France region, and few Acadians come from there. Furthermore, in the seventeenth and eighteenth centuries, before public schooling became the norm in France, the ability to read and write in French was limited to a relatively small elite that was usually "bilingual." They spoke and wrote "standard" French (the language of administration, the courts, officialdom and literature), but they also spoke a form of the language that was unique to their region. The language of the Church and universities was, at the time, largely a form of Latin and was therefore totally foreign to most ordinary people: Mass was said in that latin de cuisine, "kitchen Latin," until the 1960s. The national hymn of Acadians, the "Ave Maris Stella" is still sung in Latin today.

What Acadians brought with them originally was language, expressions and ways of pronouncing words particular mainly to central-western France. Isolation kept some old features alive, such as the verb forms "j'avions" and "j'étions" and the sounds "tch" (as in *tchai*, for "quai" meaning wharf) and "ou" (as in *houmard*, for *homard*, lobster). An *écureuil* (squirrel) was *un étchureau*; *chatouiller* (to tickle) was *pigouiller* (a word found in the Marais Poitevin area of France); to scream as loud as you could was "hucher." Some words then came from Indian languages, such as *madouesse* (porcupine) and *mache quoui* (white birch).

The problem was not the quality of Acadian French, which is described by all visitors prior to 1900 as rich, funny and varying in its music and flavour from community to community. It was the fact that, without adequate schools, and surrounded by a huge and largely hostile Anglo-American majority, little could be added to the language during the late nineteenth and early twentieth centuries, at the very time France developed its public school system on a large scale in fields typical of modern industrial cultures. What Acadians spoke, and still speak, is no better and no worse than what is spoken elsewhere, provided it is clearly taught in schools that there are several types of French, which vary from familiar usage to standardized international forms, and that they are not necessarily interchangeable. It is unlikely that Wayne Gaudet or Camille Thériault would communicate much in an international francophone gathering by speaking "chiac"!

It is not easy to catch up with the past, however. Even though after the 1970s many Acadian schools became francophone schools (with English as a second language), the level of written French is still often poor. The reason for achieving a good level of standard French is not obvious to teenagers drowned in mass American culture, and very often teachers need to retrain themselves to be able to teach in French as a first, and not a second language. Progress is slow, but constant and necessary. Acadians have all the reasons needed to be proud of their French, which has been used by several writers in literary works over the last century, but they know that contacts with the rest of the world will be made either in English or in a more standard form of French, with an Acadian flavour that will always be there, either in the accent or the choice of words.

The development of standard French for schools has benefited from the increased quality of teachers, the support of various organizations and institutions, including the federal government and cultural assistance from France, and the hard-earned goodwill of provincial governments.

Modernizing Acadian French is not the issue here—ancient words will survive or disappear along with the traditional Acadian community. The issue is to provide Acadians with the means to develop their ability to use a form of French that will, along with their own Acadian French, enable them to broaden their horizons without feeling that their own culture is always second to another. It is a major challenge, particularly in regions where many younger people switch to English as soon as the school doors close behind them, simply because the community does not offer enough opportunities (bookstores, libraries) to read material of interest to them in French, to listen to music in French (TV programs, local radio, music programs) or to enjoy social relations in their own language, or because of a still overwhelming presence of English on the world wide web. Acadian organizations, teachers, community leaders, politicians, parents and others are trying to find ways to develop their communities and their schools, to preserve and develop language, literature and music, and to reach a balance between modern and traditional values, which were largely transmitted orally. Francophones of recent origin have to defend themselves against "Frenglish," one form being the chiac or anglicized French, used by Acadians around Moncton. Schooling, in French, becomes more than ever, for a minority, an essential base for balanced bilingualism.

Survival is important, but development is also essential. New words are needed all the time and knowledge is rapidly increasing. If Acadians want their linguistic heritage to survive despite the pressures it faces from other languages, they have to rely more and more on electronic media, on institutions of their own, on connections with the francophone world, and on the pride in themselves that will lead them to consider French as their first language. For a community exposed to heavy anglicization in the past, the challenge remains enormous.

A key element in facing this challenge is to be present when public policy is put together, so that Acadian rights are protected. Acadians may disagree on their relationship with Quebec—some Nova Scotia Acadians feel constitutional changes have little to offer them, while New Brunswick Acadians feel more supportive of their Quebec neighbours-but what they should not disagree upon is the fact that Acadian rights are as dependent upon their clear recognition at the national level as they are in provincial policies.

IV. Music and Dance

Acadians love to dance and sing. Among Cajuns, music and some forms of dance (from the two-step to the quadrille) were largely responsible for the preservation of French within the American melting pot. In the 1984 novel *Les Portes Tournantes* (Revolving Doors)—from which a Franco-Canadian movie later nominated as best foreign film for an Academy Award in 1988 was made—Jacques Savoie, himself a musician and founder of the folk-rock group Beausoleil Broussard, gives us an image of many an Acadian family when he describes the Beaumont family concerts: "Every night, my father would take his fiddle out and play reels for us. It was our dessert. As we were fourteen, and not very rich, we played music

Johny Comeau, fiddle player with Les Méchants Maquereaux

Gervais (Jarvis) Benoît, fiddle player.

instead of eating…it was louder and cost less. One of my brothers played the spoons; others used what they could find.... One day, my mother stopped playing, right in the middle of a piece. My turn had come." Fiddle players abound in the different Acadian regions. One of the best known is Johny Comeau, an Acadian from Nova Scotia who has played around Canada with the folk-rock group Beausoleil Broussard and with Acadian actress Viola Léger before starting a new group, Les Méchants Maqueraux, well known throughout the Maritimes. Young Daniel Leblanc, from Baie Sainte-Marie, follows in his footsteps with a more "jazzy" approach after a stay in California, playing now with a group called "Grand Dérangement." For years the Halifax community has known Gervais ("Jarvis") Benoît, originally from Isle Madame, as a brilliant fiddler.

However, American and Scottish influences are usually obvious, and very little has remained of a French musical heritage. Baie Sainte-Marie Acadians have been heavily influenced by bluegrass because of their trading ties with the United States. They can put French words to the music, though, as the group Les Tymeux de la Baie started to do in the 1970s. Chéticamp Acadians play reels and music of Irish and Scottish origin. Everywhere in Acadie, (like in the Gaspé region)

MARTINE JACQUOT

Les Tymeux de la Baie, a country and western group.

people love country and western music, and some Acadian singers like Albert Babin have produced good country and western songs in French.

One of the reasons there was little or no instrumental music traditions is that songs brought from France were often sung, by Acadian songsters without musical accompaniment. Many songs have remained, such as "Dans les Prisons de Nantes" or "C'est À Paris, Vive le Roi!" which were sung in the evenings about France, wars and their history, giving people romantic ideas about love and nature and making "La doulce France" their ancestors had known appear pleasant, especially when seen from farms lost in freezing winter nights.

Father Anselme Chiasson of Chéticamp, a major folklorist, has indicated that Acadian songs were easily sung as *complaintes*, laments in a minor key (even songs sung in a major key in Quebec.) One of the most famous *complaintes*, written down as a poem by Frédéric À Armand Robichaud in the 1870s, is the story of *Vanilia*, a ship that left for Pointe-à-Pitre in the Antilles (French West Indies) and faced a major storm. Other complaintes were about events that marked a community, as is "Le chien à Pichi," which tells about a nineteenth-century P.E.I. Acadian who tortured his dog, actions undoubtedly

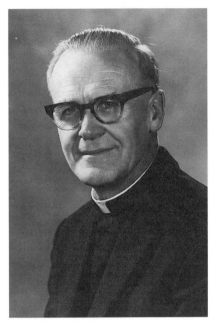

MARTINE JACQUOT

Anne-Marie Comeau as Rosalba.

Père Anselme Chiasson, an early folklorist and winner of the Grand Pré Cultural Award, 1995.

disapproved of by the other local inhabitants. Sometimes songs composed by women may deal with a caricature of some individual or with events touching the community. People in the Baie Sainte Marie, even the younger generations, remember a person with large feet as "les grands pieds de la Saumeune."

Acadian humour, obvious in the letters of Marichette, monologues of Rosalba, plays by Antonine Maillet and radio sketches of Monique Leblanc, is also abundantly present in songs. In "Sont les gens de Saulnierville," a variation on a French song, the inhabitants of that Acadian village build a boat to be manned by animals that no man except a fool would like to board! Each singer had his own repertoire, particular way of presenting songs and way of interacting with an audience.

When the twentieth century came, the time to write down or record on tape this enormous mass of oral literature had arrived, for fear of it being lost along with the old songsters. Father Anselme Chiasson collected many songs and published some, and many more were collected by Désiré d'Eon, Ronald Labelle, and English and

Folklorist Georges Arsenault.

French folklorists. Some studies have been published, like *Chansons de Shippagan* by Dominique Gauthier, or *Complaintes Acadiennes de l'Ile du Prince Edouard* by Georges Arsenault, or *La Fleur du Rosier* in N.S. The Centre d'Etudes Acadiennes at Université de Moncton and Centre Acadien at Université Sainte-Anne now gather collections and start a few much-needed publications. New songs on Acadian or other themes created in the 1920s and 1930s— "Evangéline," "Pêcheur Acadien," "Le Réveil de l'exil," "Partons la mer est belle,"—are still sung by many Acadians, who have also, however, been influenced by French and American singers of their day.

Young Acadian singers drew from that, just as they drew from the church tradition of organ playing and choirs. From the 1950s and 1960s, choirs were numerous and well-known, such as Les Chanteurs du Mascaret in Moncton, la Chorale Beauséjour, Chorales Saint-Joseph of Bathurst, or the Chorale Notre-Dame d'Acadie. Les Jeunes Chanteurs d'Acadie, won trophies in national and international contests. Now the way to reach the public, is recording CDs. Most parishes have their choirs, like Chorale LaFrance of Tracadie, Les

Alinos of Shediac or choirs of Baie Sainte-Marie or Chéticamp (L'Écho des Montagnes), that sometimes do recordings. With time, musical technique and quality have improved considerably, while retaining popular and community flavour. L'ensemble vocal Les Voix d'Acadie in Halifax is the most popular choir in N.S., celebrating 25 years of existence this year.

Young people discovered music different from their own folklore and church choirs through movements such as Les Jeunesses Musicales, which brought French Canadian artists of renown to Acadian regions in the 1960s. Academic institutions in Bathurst, Shippagan, Edmundston and elsewhere played a part in making music available to the Acadian public. By the end of the 1960s an Acadian musical revival was obviously under way, as Acadians were asserting their collective will to live modern lives while preserving their past. Old songs were rediscovered and played by young singers, composers were encouraged and festivals offered a first step to recognition in the Maritimes and elsewhere. The most brilliant career has no doubt been that of Edith Butler, from the village of Paquetville, New Brunswick, who is now among the best-known francophone singers in the world. As a young girl, with her guitar, and a ponytail, she started by singing folk songs and then blended traditional and modern material in new arrangements.

The best-known starting points for a career are sometimes provincial contests, such as the *gala de la chanson* in Caraquet, started in 1968. The list of singers and composers whose careers started there—Georges Langford (a singer from the Magdalen Islands), Edith Butler, Roseline Blanchard, Lina Boudreau, Roland Bryar, Ronald Bourgeois, Calixte Duguay, Michelle Boudreau-Samson—is endless. They often went from Caraquet or another gala in their home province (Nova Scotia had a provincial gala in the 1980s, and again from 1990) to the major French Canadian gala in Granby, Quebec. Calixte Duguay, for instance, won the Grand Prix in Granby as a composer and performer in 1974. Ronald Bourgeois had won it in 1973. Although it is important to be recognized in your own region, being recognized on a larger stage provides more opportunities for a successful career. Individual singers, backed by a group, played throughout the 1970s in places such as Maritime festivals, La Grange à Johny in Tabusintac, the *boîtes à chanson* of the northeastern shores of New Brunswick. Groups were started, the major ones being Beausoleil Broussard (which featured singer Isabelle Roy and musician-writer Jacques Savoie) and 1755, followed by Expresso SVP, Les Frotteux d'Bottes and others, ranging from folk trios to jazz

Acadian songstress Edith Butler early in her career, above. She recently received an honorary degree from Acadia University, and is shown at right with the author.

MARTINE JACQUOT

groups like the Steve Amirault Trio. The work of John Tetrault from Wolfville, N. S., Theresa Malenfant from Dieppe, or artists from elsewhere in the francophone world like Daniel Heikalo, cannot be discounted even though often more in English. A young singer like Annick Gagnon, from Grand Sault (Grand Falls) sings equally well in French and English. Even experimental rock and alternative forms has a presence, from the work of Madawaska artist Martine Michaud, to the unique songs of Zéro Degré Celsius in Moncton, the now defunct Les Oranges Bleues, La Belle Amanchure, the Glamour Puss Blues Band, and many others. Lennie Gallant, an Acadian from P.E.I. now living in Halifax, can be considered one of the top recording artists from the Maritimes.

Some Acadian singers and composers have been quite successful.

Until recently, however, they had to leave Acadie to do so. The larger market and greater opportunities led them to stay temporarily or even settle in Quebec, primarily in Montreal. Those who do not leave still face a difficult time making a living solely as artists. One of the best-known folk duos of the Argyle region of Nova Scotia, Philippe and Wendell d'Eon, never stopped working at something else, while singing on weekends in taverns, bars and festivals before deciding to give it up after a number of years.

In recent years, the hard-won ability to finance new recordings through federally-aided programs (reserved for Quebec artists until then) has enabled a large number of Acadian artists to record CDs and strengthen their ability to tour in the Maritimes and abroad for an ever growing public, although the Quebec market still remains largely closed to francophone artists form outside the province. In the case of some, this situation led them to come back to their Acadie.

Ronald Bourgeois, whose song "L'Etranger" was a hit throughout French Canada, became solidly installed in Montreal, where he worked as musical director for radio station CHGM before coming back to Nova Scotia where he started singing again while working as show producer. Angèle Arsenault played the organ for years in her small P.E.I. church before eventually leaving for Quebec. Her first two records were among the best-selling records ever—funny songs that deal with the problems experienced by women in everyday life. Born in 1943, she created a number of hits, such as "Evangéline, Acadian Queen," and her 1979 LP "Libre," was named top seller that year by the Quebec recording industry association (ADISQ). She has played the part of "La Bolduc" in a solo musical, and now records more unique songs, back in her P. E. I. home.

Calixte Duguay, a poet and composer from the Acadian peninsula has now reached in Acadian popular music the status that a Gilles Vigneault or Félix Leclerc holds in Quebec, although he was only born in 1939. Starting life as an educator at the college at Bathurst after his studies at Université Laval in Quebec City, he has been recognized as a poet (publishing *Les Stigmates du silence* in 1975), a composer of musicals ("Louis Mailloux," 1980; "La Lambique," 1983) and a TV show host on the Radio-Canada Moncton show "Encore debout." Although his musical style is not always the type younger people usually listen to, he proved that he can put on a show in 1988 when, after his own show with Lina Boudreau, he produced "Aujourd'hui pour demain" with several French Canadian artists from outside Quebec, and then went on to a new production of Louis Mailloux for the 1994 Congrès Mondial in Moncton. He has been

Calixte Duguay, singer and poet.

hired as musical director for the 1998 "Revue Musicale Acadienne" in Nova Scotia.

Some singers have reached less national and international prominence because they stayed in their own regions, such as Donat Lacroix, whose songs have been especially linked to the Acadian peninsula, Eric Surette, who is well known in southwestern Nova Scotia, Georges Langford, Raymond Breau, Etienne Deschênes,

Singer and songwriter Eric Surette.

Natasha St. Pier, Daniel Lewis, André Aucoin, Danny Boudreau, Jeannine Boudreau, Denis Richard, Mario Lebreton, Sylvia Lelièvre, and so many others. Acadian culture is to a large extent a musical culture, where an instrument or song is never far away, and where a tune often calls for a dance! Raynald Basque combines a career as visual artist with a career in music: he comes from a family known for its skits and sketches throughout New Brusnwick. Acadian singer-composers bring something new to the French song repertoire, the most successful in France having been Madawaska-born Roch Voisine, whose "Hélène" has been a major best-selling song.

To be heard, however, is another question, which reveals how vital communication networks are to a culture. Can a young musician today fight against the trend towards videos? How is it possible to produce records? Where can the money be found? A major talent, such as Ulysse Landry, a poet and remarkable guitar player, took 20 years to do a recording, even though, some of his tunes can be heard in movies—*J'avions 375 ans*, for instance. His CD, *Prendre le Temps*, was one of the Acadian nominees for the East Coast Music Awards in 1998, along with a CD by the group Loup Noir, songs from the Argyle region of Nova Scotia, and the music of *Evangéline*. The award went to Michelle Boudreau-Samson's *Libérée*. Some artists such as Roland Bryar, have produced videos that have had limited distribution; others, like Acadian peninsula musician Cayouche have built a following on the ever-popular "Rebel" and "Little Guy" feeling, mixing popular Acadian speech. Multi-media shows, like "Fièvre de nos mains" in Moncton in May 1998, bring together visual arts, song, and poetry, a blend that often interests a larger public through radio broadcasts.

Acadian artists know that, to be really successful, they need to reach larger audiences. Quality is important, and an impressive number of Acadian artists have it. Around a seasoned young musician of Franco-Manitoban origin, Patrice Boulianne, young Acadian musicians like Len Leblanc, from Nova Scotia, founded the group Blou, now touring schools regularly. Combined talents of composer Scott Macmillan and Acadian artists have enabled Symphony Nova Scotia to give Acadian concerts every year from 1993. Roland Gauvin, Johny Comeau, and Jack Gautreau are solid musicians whose talent blossoms now in the popular group Les Méchants Maquereaux. P. E. I. group Barachois combines very effectively, for French and English audiences alike, theatrical effects, traditional music from the Veillées and various forms of modern music. It is not enough, however. Nor are awards sufficient. Lina Boudreau, who collected several major awards at Caraquet and Granby, the Étoiles Du Maurier 1980 award and the Aurèle-Séguin award for best francophone composer-performer from outside Quebec, and had a part in the joint France-Québec "Starmania" rock musical, is still only in the first stages of a very promising career pursued most of the time from

The musical group Barachois, from P.E.I..

Montreal. Acadian artists do not necessarily forget the Maritimes. It remains present in their songs, and they often come back, through TV shows or for concert tours, particularly: Marie-Jo Thério, an actress and singer from Moncton, has even written a song in "Chiac" (the French spoken in Moncton) on her first CD, which led her to increased international recognition. A major artist like Marcel Aymar, from Baie Sainte-Marie, considers his Acadian identity essential, even though he worked mostly in Ontario and in Quebec.

Bringing a group together, recording and touring requires an enormous amount of money; the limits of the Maritime market are severe and "regional" artists were until recently considered inferior by promoters and show organizers. Despite these obstacles, groups and young composers emerge all the time. Music fans look forward to a gathering of shows during "Contact-Acadie," which takes place in

Arthur LeBlanc, violin prodigy.

Moncton every year. Regionally produced programs on Maritime or national TV networks and community radio make them better known. Beausoleil Broussard was the first group to do a whole LP in Acadian regions. Several studios exist in Dieppe, in Yarmouth, in Edmundston. Collective shows like the ones done for August 15 in Caraquet, or "L'Acadie en Fête" in N. S., have brought recognition to a large number of artists.

In the classical field, first-rate musicians have emerged who have not forgotten their Acadian roots. Anna Malenfant, born in Shediac in 1905, became a well-known opera singer after moving to Hartford, Boston and Montreal. From 1944, as Marie Lebrun, she recorded a number of Acadian songs as well. Arthur LeBlanc, born in Saint-Anselme in 1906, became an internationally renowned violinist. His father had first taught him how to play; he then moved on to Quebec, Boston, and then Paris, where he played in the Orchestre Symphonique de Paris from 1935 to 1936. Back in Canada he played and taught music in Quebec City and Montreal. He performed for radio and television and composed works, in particular, "Petite suite canadienne." After his death in 1985, Université de Moncton took his name for its resident string quartet in 1988. Benoît Poirier had a long career as an organist. Rose-Marie Landry, born in Timmins, Ontario in 1946 but raised in Caraquet, started a brilliant career after studies in Quebec and in France, singing with the Winnipeg Symphony, the Tudor ensemble of Montreal and the Calgary Festival Chorus, among others.

Other brilliant vocalists include Robert Savoie, from Lamèque, New Brunswick, a world renowned baritone; Eugène Lapierre, from Prince Edward Island; and Laura Gaudet, Marie-Germaine and Marguerite LeBlanc. Gloria Richard (born 1934), a soprano who studied in Moncton and Montreal, worked with several symphonies from Halifax to Winnipeg. Here, as in other fields, children of Acadie come back to the Maritimes, rich with experience gathered elsewhere, from which future generations may benefit.

Through the initiative of organizer Mathieu Duguay, the small village of Lamèque, where people live off fishing and the peat moss industry, each year welcomes a baroque music festival with international guests, and many world-renowned musicians take part. The small parish of Saint-Bernard in Nova Scotia is offering a series of concerts every summer, and no visitor to Edmundston can miss Les petits violons de Saint-Basile.

Acadian step-dancing, square dances and other forms of dance have always been loved. However, partly because the Catholic Church viewed dancing as dangerous, many old French dances have been forgotten, although some are still found in the Chéticamp area. Today some groups offer folk dancing in the Acadian tradition, such as Les danseurs de la Vallée Saint-Jean, Les Feux Chalins, Les danseurs Evangéline, and La Baie en Joie from Baie Sainte-Marie, (the creation of Anne-Marie Comeau, also known for her "Rosalba" monologues). It is often a blend of tap dancing and reinvented folk dances with Acadian themes. Barbara LeBlanc has studied carefully old Acadian dances, and gives regular workshops on them. Reviving old traditions like "danser les quatre" is part of preserving an Acadian identity for the future.

Although there are no world-famous classical dancers in Acadie, Chantal Cadieux has in the 1990s created, with Dansencorps, the first modern dance troupe, based in Moncton. The troupe Tempdem is a dance school in the Acadian peninsula. In the Baie Sainte-Marie, Charelle Thibault, who taught at the Royal Winnipeg Ballet, is well known as a choreographer and dance instructor.

The best-known Acadian ballet dancer was Jeannine Léger, who was from 1957 one of the dancers in the Les Grands Ballets Canadiens.

V. Folklore

Folklore is not only songs. It is also oral tradition, folktales, oral history. It is traditional festivals and knowledge of how to build houses, how to build fences and barns, and how to view the world. For a long time, Acadian culture was essentially based on oral tradition.

Acadian folktales are abundant. In each community was at least one individual who would tell tales during winter nights when Acadians led a life guided by the seasons. Some of these tales have been collected and published. They include the story of "L'Oiseau de la Vérité" (The Bird of Truth) and tales of ghost ships, pirates and bootleggers. One of the characters who frequently appears in Acadian folktales is Ti-Jean, a small individual who is able to trick giants and other people using his sharp intelligence. The same character can be found in stories from Louisiana, and writer Melvin Gallant created a book with a number of those tales that is now widely read in Acadian schools.

Acadian folklore can be an object of study as well as a focus for tourists. Since 1966 Université de Moncton has provided an Acadian folklore course, and the folklore centre there is managed by Ronald Labelle, who has published, in particular, a study of a Memramcook area village called *Au Village du Bois,* collections of songs, and a fascinating study of Chezzetcook Ouest and Grand-Désert, the only Acadian community from the 1760s close to Halifax. Riches are held in early collections, starting with *Chez les anciens Acadiens, causeries du grand-père Antoine* by André-Thadé Bourque in 1911. One can read *Légendes des Iles de la Madeleine* by Anselme Chiasson, *Shippagan, Anecdotes, tours et légendes* by Francis Savoie, *La littérature orale de la Baie Sainte-Marie* by Alain Doucet, and *Ti-Jean* by Melvin Gallant.

One interesting folklore collector, Sister Catherine Jolicoeur, a primary school teacher and coordinator of a folklore project for Laval University, published some of the 35,000 Acadian legends she gathered in *Les Plus belles légendes acadiennes,* 1981. Antonine Maillet wrote a thesis on Acadian proverbs, and Félix Thibodeau created several books in the Acadian language of the Baie Sainte-Marie dealing with daily chores and community events. Désiré d'Eon, founder of *Le Courrier de la Nouvelle-Ecosse,* published several legends in this weekly over the years. Much folklore has also been published and written in *L'Evangéline.*

Acadie had one of the richest and longest-lasting oral tradition in

Félix Thibodeau, educator, writer, craftsman and storyteller.

North America. And this is still the case to some extent. Acadian writers of today know what they owe that tradition, which has still not been fully explored. Antonine Maillet has said that she was the last of the tellers of tales and the first of the novelists, and poet Gérald Leblanc decided to become a writer because his grandfather was a storyteller. Acadian folk tales (apart from those brought from France that all cultures knew in the eighteenth century, such as "Little Red Riding Hood," "Tom Thumb," and other universal folk tales with social warnings) brought to life a rich imagery, a landscape alive with goblins (*les lutins*) and will-o'-the-wisps (*les feux-follets*), ghost ships and hidden treasure. How many Acadians hid treasures and crocks of silver before being deported? Legends have it that some returned and found them again, all around Noel shore on the Bay of Fundy, for instance.

Legends also dealt with particular times in Acadian life that held special value. The *Mi-Carême* was not only a celebration that took place to break the fasting period during Lent; it was a terrifying creature that stole children when they did not sleep past bedtime, a function she shared with *Bonhomme Sept-Heures* and the terrible

Désiré d'Eon, folklorist and founder of Le Courrier.

Gougou in the Baie des Chaleurs area. Which child would not have been afraid when fearsome characters like those, or the Gippettes, the Gypsies or the Wandering Jew, roamed at night? The last two were the creations of a Catholic culture that kept alive racial clichés found elsewhere. They were no less terrifying! This imaginary world could hold devils, ghosts and bogeymen, but it could also provide marvellous ways of transportation—the *chasse-galerie*, invented by French Canadians at the time they worked far away from normal social life in chantiers, logging camps, for Acadians became a way to fly to social events, and not only for humans! The devil was used as a warning for young girls, at least until the end of the nineteenth century. It was usual to find him associated with the dangers of dancing, particularly in dance halls.

Legends, tell us much about Acadians of old. If a legend was made to warn against dances on Good Friday, it is probably because some Acadians did not hesitate to bring a mouth organ and liquor where they could dance, devil or not. There were witches and haunted houses. Priests could perform incredible miracles, like the one who changed a glass of gin into a glass of milk, or the one whose blessing changed the direction of the wind to save a house from fire. It was life in a country where many fishermen needed protection—the *Vanilia* was only one of many ships saved by the Blessed Virgin. How would children not automatically be given a first name of Marie or Joseph, when the Virgin and Saint Joseph were present in so many Acadian legends? Children of today may not believe in the "sur-natchettes" any longer, but they will discover them in a show by P.E.I. writer Paul D. Gallant, now working from Chéticamp.

Acadian regions were also rich with anecdotes, which sometimes found their ways into songs, books or plays. In a country where people easily gave each other nicknames to avoid ambiguous similarities of first and last names, any unusual feature of an individual automatically begged attention. Anecdotes are about healers with mysterious powers, teeth-pullers, and strong men and women. Books for children from the Baie Sainte-Marie celebrate Adolphe à Nicolas, whom everybody saw going around with his cart, or Cy à Mateur, called "Sail à Majeur" in an Edith Butler song, who was able to travel faster than the wind.

Réjean Aucoin picked a character from the Chéticamp area, the fast postman Johny à Minou, to create *Le Tapis de Grand-Pré*, which was broadcast on the radio and made into a book illustrated by poet and visual artist Herménégilde Chiasson and translated into English. Lawrence Meuse of Sainte-Anne du Ruisseau in the District of Argyle, Nova Scotia, has written about nineteenth-century characters such as La Taube, Bouillon and La Ruiquinne, preserving them for future generations. The mystery of Jérôme, a man left on the shores of Baie Sainte-Marie without legs, inspired Germaine Comeau to write a play and provided Phil Comeau with the subject of a feature film, *Le Secret de Jérôme.*

Nova Scotia author Germaine Comeau.

The riches of Acadian oral tradition, luckily preserved in memories and folklore centres, has only been skimmed by artists, who can discover through it a new understanding of the Maritime space.

VI. Literary Arts

With a rich heritage, a history worthy of epics, varied regions to explore and describe, and a powerful imagination, Acadians had everything they needed to create a unique and fascinating literature.

They also had many difficulties in creating one, despite the fact that the first literary creations in French in North America took place at Port-Royal in the early 1600s. The problems were obvious. Lack of education, in particular, led to a paucity of writing skills. Not so long ago, statistics indicated that even in the 1980s the majority of Acadians had no more than a seventh grade.

So, although a small group had benefited from instruction and advanced cultural, technical and professional skills, the large majority of Acadians suffered from literacy problems. These difficulties were reinforced by the fact that, even late in the twentieth century, a number of textbooks for Acadian schools were in English.

Books by French founders and visitors of the seventeenth and eighteenth centuries, even when known, related the "old" Acadie and did not provide nineteenth-or twentieth-century Acadians with models they could follow. Most often they were out of print and are only slowly being reprinted and rediscovered now. Some of them, starting with the romantic views of l'abbé Raynal, are quite far removed from Acadian reality, even when attempting to describe it. There were legends and tales, and all that Acadians told from generation to generation, but this was oral, and in which language should it be written down? Should it be in Acadian French, using a phonetic system to write it down as it was told, or in standard French, often considered by the elite as the only way to prove that Acadians were as good as others in the "purity" of their language? There were models, but they were not Acadian—they were French or French Canadian authors.

Literature, when it finally started, proved to be one of the important elements in defining an Acadian identity. The newspaper *Le Moniteur Acadien* was a major boost for literary arts, not only because it provided space for writing, but because it deliberately encouraged Acadians to write in French for the whole world to read. Articles, letters, tales, dialogues—that newspaper and others offered a service that cannot be forgotten, at a time when the very idea of publishing was alien to an essentially oral community. Times, however, were not very open to the acceptance of Acadian French. Marichette, a school mistress from Memramcook named Emilie Leblanc, taught in Acadian regions of Nova Scotia and wrote letters to *L'Evangéline* from 1895 to 1898 in Acadian French. Witty and brilliant, they were attacked by the Acadian establishment of the time for being too close to "vulgar" French. What was written then had to be in a "pure" form of French that unfortunately, did not reflect what people actually spoke or listened to.

When Pascal Poirier stated that Acadian French was the language of French Renaissance poet Ronsard, he may have been correct about what Ronsard himself spoke (and we have little knowledge of that), but he was not very scientific in saying so. What he wanted to say was that Acadian French is a form of French that has its own interest and importance. Acadians have no reason not to be proud of their language. Even Monctonians speaking chiac, the language of the utterly mixed bilingual, prove that it exists and, if only for that reason, would be interesting to read and use in literature.

Acadian literature which started with Lescarbot in the 1600s, was needed to give the community a vision of what it was. Theatre and poetry—from the 1960s in particular—were to provide that vision, without complacency and without resorting to the use of folklore and history as their sole subjects.

History, however, has been important and still is: the success of an historical novel such as *Le Feu du mauvais temps* by Claude LeBouthillier, published in 1989, followed by *Les Marées du Grand Dérangement* and the historical chronicles collected as *Pour l'honneur de mon prince* by Robert Pichette in 1990, are a clear indication of that. We now have guides to historical sites in the old and the new Acadie, thanks to work undertaken by Fernand de Varenne, who published a rich volume, *Lieux et monuments historiques de l'Acadie*, in 1987 or Yves Cormier, with *L'Acadie des Maritimes* in 1992. None of these would have been possible without modern Acadian publishers. Claude LeBouthillier, who now works with a major Quebec publisher, started with three novels put out by Les Editions d'Acadie, founded in Moncton in 1972 as a small publishing house by a group of writers and university professors. Robert Pichette, who released two books of poetry with the same publisher, was later published by short-lived Michel Henry Editeur, founded in the 1980s by a former manager of Les Editions d'Acadie. Fernand de Varenne's book, beautifully printed and illustrated would not have been done had not Les Editions d'Acadie grown to become one of the largest publishers in the Maritimes, with increasing ties to francophone publishers elsewhere, from Quebec to Senegal.

Francophone historians, poets and novelists interested in Acadie were at first from elsewhere—France or Quebec. The views of the first French-Canadian historian, François-Xavier Garneau, in the 1840s, were that Acadians were primarily a doomed community with a tragic past. Gradually, though, Acadian historians started to record and interpret their own history. Placide Gaudet was one of those. Born in Cap-Pelé in 1850, he started teaching after having studied at the Collège Saint-Joseph. A journalist for several newspapers in the late nineteenth century, he later became archivist for the National Archives in Ottawa in 1899. A major researcher on Acadian history and genealogy, he published in 1922, eight years before his death, a study called *Le Grand Dérangement*. Before Placide Gaudet, Acadians knew little about their own history. He opened up new dimensions for his people, and all Acadians owe him a major debt.

A former graduate of Université de Moncton, Régis Brun, born at Cap-Pelé in 1937, has changed our outlook on Acadians with his studies of them as a people (*De Grand-Pré À Kouchibouguac*, 1982), of pioneer of the new Acadie Joseph Guogen (*Pionnier de la Nouvelle-Acadie*, 1984) and of fishing in southeastern New Brunswick. He also wrote literary texts, one on sorcery and witchcraft in Acadie (*La Mariecomo*, 1974) and one on growing up on a small Acadian village in the 1950s. He is one of those who, with Maurice Basque (now director of the Centre d'Etudes Acadiennes in Moncton) and Jacques-Paul Couturier in Edmundston, changes our vision of Acadians to a dynamic North American community, however much no one can minimize the hardships it had to endure.

It is fundamentally necessary for history to be reread by Acadian eyes, largely because a good number of things in that history were transmitted orally, leaving much leeway for interpretation. Father Clarence d'Entremont, an Acadian from West Pubnico who worked in Louisiana and New England and was an active nationalist, has produced massive studies on Nicolas Denys and on the French colony at Cap-Sable in the seventeenth and eighteenth centuries, along with local histories on Pubnico and Wedgeport. Alphonse Deveau has published many books on the Baie Sainte-Marie area, starting with *La Ville Française*, in which he points out how unfortunate, in a way, it was for Acadians to have settled in villages and not to have founded a major urban centre. Léon Thériault, who teaches at Université de Moncton, has been actively involved in political analyses of Acadian history, and his book *Le Pouvoir en Acadie* called for greater "French power" and better consciousness of collective goals, proposing for New Brunswick an approach similar to Belgium—two communities, interrelated but with a number of separate structures. Father Anselme Chiasson documented the whole history of Chéticamp, from folk traditions to chores of daily life, making his monograph a model of what should be done for all Acadian villages and is now being done increasingly in one form or another by local historians. Neil Boucher studied the evolution of Ile Surette for his M.A. at Acadia University, devoting his Ph.D thesis to the first Acadian bishop, Monsignor Edouard LeBlanc.

Father Clarence d'Entremont, historian.

The 1960s was marked by a desire to bring Acadians to terms with their own history, and this desire led to the founding of historical societies. The Société d'Histoire Acadienne, founded in 1960, publishes *Les Cahiers* four times a year. Société Nicolas Denys, Société historique du Madawaska, Société Historique de l'Ile-du-Prince-Edouard and similar societies in Pubnico, Chéticamp, and Ile

Madame and the Baie Sainte-Marie area are proof of great interest in their history among Acadians.

Barbara LeBlanc, an Acadian author and educator originally from the Chéticamp area who travelled to France and Italy before coming back to the Maritimes to become for a while the supervisor of the historic park in Grand Pré (and the first woman to have that position), before becoming president of the FANE, is invited regularly to talk about Acadian history, by English and French alike. At the Grand Pré park, the interpretation of Acadian history, which was limited in the 1950s and mixed with the memories of the soldiers who had expelled the Acadians, has now become more scientific and offers a more positive view of the Acadian world prior to Expulsion. The purchase of traditional lands by a joint body of the SNA (National Society of Acadians) and Heritage Canada in 1998 may finally result in development of a site devoted to Acadian archaeology and memorabilia, along with other

MARTINE JACQUOT

Barbara LeBlanc, ethnologist and former president of FANE.

developments within the area. Heritage Canada has an Acadian advisory council on which a number of historians sit.

It is important for all of us that Acadian life not be seen through rose, or dark-coloured glasses but, as documents, archives and oral tradition tell us, as it was. Lack of money and manpower and the disappearance of key witnesses from the past all conspire to make things difficult, but the achievements of Acadian historians and others writing about Acadie is impressive in quality and quantity. Some of this history will undoubtedly inspire literature. More will come out of Acadian Studies at Université de Moncton, chaired for a long time by the major historian of our literature, Marguerite Maillet. With the development of a Ph.D program in Acadian literature at the Université de Moncton, a dictionary of Acadian literary works is presently in the works.

There are also museums in Acadie: one at Université Sainte-Anne, one in Pubnico, one at Moncton, one in Caraquet, one in Edmundston. The Village Historique Acadien at Bertrand, near Caraquet is a magnificent reconstruction of life in the nineteenth century, and the Village des Pionniers Acadiens in Mont-Carmel, P.E.I. also recalls the Acadian past. An Acadian historical village for Nova Scotia is being put together in Pubnico, the oldest continuously Acadian community in the Maritimes. Graveyards can tell many stories of people forgotten, such as the old graveyard on the *platain* in Chéticamp or the graveyard in Tignish, P.E.I., with its mix of Irish and Acadian names.

More Acadian authors have been published during the last forty years than ever before. Poetry nights, and the arts and literature on the airwaves of Radio-Canada, reveal that there are now four generations of Acadian poets at work. An Acadian literature is taking shape, and that Acadian literature does much more than celebrate the past.

Until recently, there was not much of a network of bookstores and retail points through which Acadian authors could reach their market. This is now gradually taking shape. What a writer needs most, though, is the will to communicate a unique message to the community, sending back to it a particular vision of itself. But how to do this, when one has no models? For Acadian writers, until recently, the only models were from France or Quebec. Writers who emerged in the 1970s were suddenly amazed to be considered authors. All writers who emerged then, and Antonine Maillet and a few who started their careers earlier, such as Léonard Forest who was both a poet and a filmmaker, were not only writing their own works, but were creating precedents, inventing a tradition and opening the way for Acadian literature. It is only in the 1990s that a new generation has emerged to define itself in relation to those elders, who are still very much active.

There had been writers and poets before the 1960s, but however important they are, the sincere nationalist lyrics of Father Napoléon Landry from Sainte-Marie de Kent (1884-1956), author of *Poèmes de mon pays* and *Poèmes acadiens*, or the poems of Joséphine Duguay (1896-1981) published in *L'Evangéline*, make it hard to consider that they open up any kind of tradition. They are imitations of French verse, with images of Acadie to match the author's feelings—indeed, Académie Française recognized the poetry of Napoléon Landry with an award in 1955.

For Acadians, it was necessary to go back to the roots, not only to the Acadian language, but to the realization that the Acadian language was the expression of a community of mostly poor, hard-working and not very literate people who nevertheless had a lot of humour, loved to drink and dance and frolic, and whose fundamental quality was good sense. But how do you write in Acadian French, a language that was largely unwritten? Each author wrote down his own brand of Acadian and lived with it.

The first to give Acadian French literary value through her work is Antonine Maillet, with plays such as *La Sagouine* (1968), *Les Crasseux, Evangéline Deusse*, and in total more than thirty plays and novels. Her first plays, recognized by several awards as early as 1958, and her first novel, *Pointe-aux-Coques* (1960), were written in "standard" French, following fairly traditional patterns. Maillet realized that a classical literary approach would never reveal what was unique to her country, Acadie (primarily the Acadian villages of New Brunswick's southeastern coast), and that she needed to create her own particular form of literary expression to reveal that unique character. Despite a lack of publishers in Acadian regions when she started, and despite the fact that publishers in Montreal were at first not terribly interested in her work, she gradually became a major world author without renouncing her basic goal—to give the world a vision of Acadie, particularly the Acadie of the thirties, when bootleggers, male and female, wreaked havoc and made fortunes along the coasts by trafficking with Quebec, the West Indies and the United States. She relied heavily on oral history to enrich her work, but she is not simply interpreting folklore. Her characters are powerful, vibrant, ribald and full of energy, such as the female bootleggers Maria à Gélas in the novel *Mariaagélas* (1973). She brings to life figures like Jeanne de Valois, a major forerunner of French education in New Brunswick, as well as more universal symbols like the Chemin Saint-Jacques, where Acadian reality mixes with medieval symbols.

Maillet rewrote the story of the Expulsion in a novel of the return of Acadians to their land, *Pélagie-la-Charrette*, which earned her the Goncourt award as best French novelist of the year in 1979. She has given Acadians a positive, pleasant and ribald vision of themselves that is quite the opposite of the sad Evangelines of Longfellow's heritage.

Few authors have been celebrated as much during their lifetime. The Prix Goncourt was only one in a long list of awards and honorary degrees. Antonine Maillet is one of the few authors in Acadie and Quebec who successfully live off their writing. She had to live in Montreal to achieve this, although she comes back regularly to her lighthouse near Bouctouche. Université de Moncton recognized her immense contribution to Acadian letters by organizing a conference on her work in 1989 and naming her chancellor of the university. France recognized her importance by naming her to the Haut Conseil de la Francophonie, an advisory body to former French president Mitterrand.

Other Acadian authors who chose to write in Acadian French may not be as well-known or as successful, but since the 1970s they have provided us with an important link between what Acadians actually speak and what becomes literary, through their stories, monologues, songs and plays. Félix Thibodeau has written many dialogues in Baie Sainte-Marie Acadjonne French, usually about events between modern fictitious characters. He also rewrote Napoléon Bourassa's novel *Jacques et Marie* under the title *La Pierre Magique*. Lorraine Diotte, also a popular singer known in her region as "La Bolduc Acadienne," has offered us tasty satires of society through the character of Polidore, a poor Acadian worker from the northeastern shores of New Brunswick. Rosalba graced the Baie Sainte-Marie with her monologues even before La Sagouine existed. Albert "Ti-Phonse" Belzile, from Madawaska, is known for his comical sketches and monologues. The tradition of satirical monologues in Acadie is so rich that Monique Leblanc, a young writer of the 1980s, often starts her radio broadcasts with a monologue dealing with present-day problems.

Some poets of the 1970s such as Raymond LeBlanc and Guy Jean have used Acadian French to express what they felt standard literary French could not. Authors such as Gérald Leblanc, have decided to build their work around the mix of English and French that is the reality of being Acadian around Moncton. *Éloge du chiac* (1995), poems and the memories-novel *Moncton Mantra* (1998) exemplify this desire. Poets who became known in the 1960s, such as Léonard Forest and Ronald Després, are highly lyrical, and their Acadie is somewhere between loves, dreams and the realities of regions where they could not live because they had to leave and work elsewhere.

The 1970s were the age of revolt and open expression of new dimensions. Raymond Leblanc with his first book in 1972, *Cri de Terre* (Land-Cry); Ulysse Landry with his songs and poems; Herménégilde Chiasson, whose poem "Eugénie Melanson" marks clearly how much young Acadians must look to a different future; Gérald Leblanc; Rose Després with her harsh, wild surrealism; Dyane Léger; and Albert Roy. All look for new ways to express Acadie. Far from the land or the marvels of the past, this is the Acadie of young people who leave universities and wish to have equal treatment in

Acadian poets and musicians meet with Belgian writers in 1993. L-R: Henri-Dominique Paratte, Herménégilde Chiasson, Marcia Babineau, Gérald LeBlanc, Albert Roy, Daniel Heikalo and Eric Brogniet.

their own society without having to assimilate. It is an Acadie that wants its share of power, calls for an Acadian territory and discovers how much must be done before such a territory can be organized within the Canadian system. It is an Acadie that became known in all francophone countries in the 1980s.

Poets are often involved in other forms of art as well: Calixte Duguay is a singer as well as a poet, starting in the *boîtes à chansons* on New Brunswick's northern shores in the 1960s before becoming world-famous. Herménégilde Chiasson, a visual artist before he became a poet, worked with Radio-Canada and is now primarily a filmmaker. Gérald Leblanc authored several plays. Léonard Forest was the first Acadian filmmaker as well as one of its first poets. Poets often have another job, as anywhere else: Raymond LeBlanc teaches philosophy, Guy Jean and Ronald Després work for the federal government, Germaine Comeau works at Université Sainte-Anne.

The most successful novelist after Antonine Maillet, is Jacques Savoie, now in his forties, who won several awards and whose second novel, *Les Portes Tournantes* (1984) (Revolving Doors) was shot as a joint France-Canada production in 1988. Too "artistic" to win wide public support in France or an Academy Award, it shows Campbellton as it was in the 1930s and portrays one of the most unforgettable modern child heroes in the French language. Savoie, who works regularly for television, had another novel, *Raconte-Moi Massabielle* (1980), made into a movie a few years before. Written in Acadian French it reveals how small villages built at the turn of the century or during the construction of the railway became obsolete, in decline and threatened by large mining companies and by the invasion of mass U.S. culture. Savoie now expresses himself in more international prose. With six novels, several other books, plays, scripts and participation in international projects, he is one of the most dynamic Acadian artists. *L'Actualité*, the major Quebec magazine, chose him as one of the most important young "Québécois," proving that Acadian artists could be accepted for their work in the Québécois artistic milieu. He is now involved in script writing in Moncton and Québec.

MARTINE JACQUOT

Dyane Léger, poet and visual artist.

Recreating past Acadies, novelists have thrown light on forgotten events in their regions, rediscovered history and created unique characters. Here the work of the novelist often connects with that of the historian. Louis Haché and Jeannine Landry-Thériault have solidly grounded their work in the Acadian peninsula in New Brunswick. Haché has focused on reviving history as seen by ordinary people, such as the fights for fishermen's unions in *Un Cortège d'anguilles*. Landry-Thériault is more intimate in her approach, portraying women characters who want to escape small, tightly-knit communities in which it is impossible to realize one's dreams.

Claude LeBouthillier, also from the Acadian peninsula, has produced, with *Le Feu du Mauvais Temps*, a major historical novel blending past and present, Acadie and France, for readers in all francophone countries. He followed this major saga with *Les Marées du Grand Dérangement* before coming back to more contemporary writing dealing with the question of Acadian identity. Born in 1946 and a professional psychologist, living in Quebec but coming back to

Caraquet regularly, he previously opened up new territory for Acadian readers with nationalistic science fiction (*L'Acadien reprend son pays*, 1977), calls for universal peace and understanding (*Isabelle-sur-mer*, 1979) and a powerful plunge into the dark recesses of the Acadian soul (*C'est pour quand le paradis*, 1989). He also chaired the national public lending rights program in Ottawa from 1987 to 1990. Melvin Gallant, teacher and publisher, now living in the Dominican Republic, is also a poet and a novelist. His novel *Le chant des grenouilles* (Frog's Song) won the France-Acadie award. His essays, often blending photography and text, such as in *Le Pays d'Acadie* (The Country of Acadie), and his texts for children have been translated into English. He has also acted as historian, with a new edition of the diary of Dièreville, and organized the first textbook for Acadian schools produced by francophone Maritime specialists, *Les Maritimes*.

Régis Brun, an accomplished historian, has chronicled the life of a teenager in an Acadian village of the 1950s with *Cap-Lumière*, also presented as a series of monologues on Radio-Canada. The life of teenagers is also the subject of *Comme à la vraie cachette*, by Albert Roy, his fifth book, published thanks to a new publisher for the region, Les Editions Marévie, now unfortunately out of business.

Les Editions d'Acadie has enabled Christiane Saint-Pierre, originally from Quebec but living in Caraquet, to publish a series of short stories, *Sur les pas de la mer*; and a novel, *Absente pour la journée*, excerpts of which were published in the Quebec City daily *Le Devoir*. Hélène Harbec, also originally from Quebec, uses her dual identity to bring new light on the Acadian soul. Writing in Acadian French about the joys and pleasures of village life has been the trademark of Laurier Melanson, whose novel *Zélika à cochon vert* has been adapted for the stage.

Some novelists write in an unusual style. The work of France Daigle is closer to abstract paintings, film and poetry than to other historical or descriptive novels. It reveals an important side of Acadian literature and elements in the Acadian psyche in an oblique way. *Sans jamais parler du vent* was the first of many novels where structure is often more important than realism. A novelist such as Germaine Comeau, is the exact opposite. Her novel, *L'Eté aux puits secs* is very close to the reality of life along the shores of Baie Sainte-Marie. With *Loin de France*, she tries to recreate the time of Electric City in the 1900s. Unbridled humour is the trademark of plays and prose writings by Rino Morin-Rossignol, also one of the main Acadian essayists of the 1980s. With *Ippon*, Jacques Ouellette started a series of works aimed at a popular readership.

Compared to contemporary novelists, those of the 1950s such as Alphonse Deveau look less modern. French literature of the 1950s had already reached the stage of the nouveau roman, some writers were using literature to express political ideas, and Albert Camus was about to win the Nobel prize. As interesting as novels celebrating Acadian history may have been, they essentially looked towards the past along lines laid down by historical novels of the nineteenth century. It took the 1990s to have new novelists in Acadie, along with a new generation of poets: Marc Arseneau, Mario Thériault, Jean Babineau, and Serge Patrice Thibodeau (winner of the Nelligan award).

It was essential for young Acadians to see their "country," although still difficult to define, as a place where history and tradition do not prevent them from participating in contemporary forms of art and culture. It was vital because, as a minority, the whole Acadian group could easily have been cornered into surviving as little more than preservers of folklore. It was important for Acadian creators to be as good and interesting as creators anywhere else, with their particular brand of identity, more North American in many ways than their Québécois and French counterparts.

Acadians have always loved theatre. Plays by Molière filled the halls in Chéticamp and Bouctouche in the early 1900s. People were fond of *veillées* (evening performances) during which storytellers presented a small show. In the nineteenth and early twentieth centuries, some amateur companies staged the standard international repertoire. Then Acadian dramatists and more professional companies emerged. *La Sagouine* has crossed the borders of Acadie and Canada with success, and its interpreter, Viola Léger, is known worldwide. Working, for economic reasons, out of Montreal, she brought her expertise back to New Brunswick, founding her own theatre company there in the 1980s, while not renouncing her career goals elsewhere.

Other professional companies were born from the many enthusiastic amateur groups of the 1970s, particularly Le Théâtre Populaire d'Acadie based in Caraquet, and L'Escaouette in Moncton, the latter specializing in plays for teenagers. Shediac has seen new forms of summer theatre in recent years, and places such as Chéticamp have long provided plays of interest to the community. Universities played a major role in developing theatre forms. The Bathurst college when it was still in existence, Université de Moncton and Université Sainte-Anne have provided support for amateur companies that use Acadian and foreign material. Organizations such as Théâtre-Acadie in New Brunswick try to provide support for Acadian actors and plays, but life for actors is difficult at best—touring costs money, and the

MARTINE JACQUOT

Viola Léger is the actress who has brought Antonine Maillet's memorable character, La Sagouine, *to life.*

Maritime public, although polls indicate that they want to see more plays, is limited in numbers. Until recently, actors had few ways of earning money from film or advertising (a major source of income in other parts of the world) and the number of plays in which they could act was limited to a few each year. Although there is still a long way to go, and many move to Montreal to study or act, improvement will eventually come for francophone artists in the Maritimes. Some progress is also linked to the emergence of organizations like the Fédération Culturelle Canadienne-Française (FCCF), fostering exchanges with other regions of French Canada.

Some Acadians have emerged as playwrights, although the publication of plays is limited by the difficulty of selling them, except to libraries and schools. Jules Boudreau, from the Acadian peninsula, created contemporary plays as well as two plays on historical themes —*Cochu et le soleil* and *Louis Mailloux*. Laval Goupil, with *Tête d'eau* and *Le Djibou*, emerged as the major Acadian playwright of the 1970s. *Le Djibou* played to packed audiences all through the summer of 1997 in Caraquet, proving its theme could survive time. Germaine Comeau, from *Les Pêcheurs déportés* to *Jérôme*, has created plays adapted to the Bale Sainte-Marie environment, traditions and symbols. Gracia Couturier, now literary director of Les Editions d'Acadie, has created innovative themes in her plays for children, and farcical situations, such as the pregnant man in *Mon mari est un ange*. Gérald LeBlanc and Herménégilde Chiasson wrote plays for L'Escaouette, and Raymond Leblanc for the student company at Université de Moncton. Viola Léger brought together texts from Acadian poets in her show Elouèzes.

One dimension of modern theatre is radio and TV plays: people such as Germaine Comeau, Yvan Vanheck, Antonine Maillet, Jacques Savoie and many others have used this medium to reach a larger audience. Film has gradually become another tool for Acadian writers: documentary film has a 30-year old tradition in Acadie.

Acadian literature can be seen as both fairly ancient and fairly recent. It is true that Lescarbot and Nicolas Denys lived in and wrote about Acadie in the seventeenth century. However, more Acadian authors writing in French have published in the last twenty years than during the past three centuries. Twenty years ago, there were no publishers to speak of in Acadie. Today there are several publishers, among them Les Editions d'Acadie, Perce-Neige, Les Editions de la Grande Marée, and Les Editions du Grand Pré. Here as in other areas, however, it is not easy to survive, and many have disappeared after a few years. Modern Acadian literature is young but promising, and more and more courses and anthologies are devoted to it. The major book fair in Acadie, the Salon du Livre in Edmundston, gives yearly proof of this.

Although most Acadian authors are of Acadian ethnic origin, some others have chosen Acadie as the place where they write and to which they are committed. Among them are Christiane Saint-Pierre, Hélène Harbec and Denise Paquette from Quebec, Martine L. Jacquot and Pierre Gérin from France and Gérard Etienne from Haiti. These authors are not French authors writing about Acadian traditions or history, such as Jeanne Ducluzeau, who lives in France and has been published in Moncton. They have taken an active part in the Acadian renaissance of recent decades, and their outlook is from an Acadian, not a French or a Québécois point of view. Jean Péronnet from Lyon (France) has created with Pépère Goguen, one of the favourite characters of Acadian children. Some authors live in Acadie and write for a larger public, such as the late Yves Beauchesne from Quebec, who taught for a few years at Université Sainte-Anne, where an institute commemorates him.

Where does this leave authors of Acadian ethnic origin who write in English, either because they never had schooling in French or because they prefer to express themselves for the regional majority? It makes them anglophone writers of Acadian origin. Some are brilliant, and indeed write about their Acadianness in very interesting tones: Simone Poirier-Bures gave Acadians in Halifax their first novel with *Candyman*, Betty Boudreau Vaughan gave her view of life in the Baie Sainte-Marie area with *I'll Buy You an Ox*. There will always be English literature written by Acadians. Language is one of the fundamental elements of a culture, and linguistic choice is fundamental to the outlook the author takes. An authentic Maritime Acadian literature in French is an enrichment for the whole community and a powerful demonstration of the strength of the culture from which it arises.

A large number of books have been written about Acadians in English. Some are literature, some are history: this is a guide to the most important of them.

The first is H.W. Longfellow's *Evangeline*, in 1845. It has become an icon of the Acadian tragedy, exemplified by the figure of Evangeline, the young Acadian woman separated from her lover who roams all the Eastern seaboard to finally discover her lover Gabriel, dying in a hospital in Philadelphia. The story can be read as a romantic story, as a poem of the discovery of America, or as a romanticized depiction of the Acadian tragedy in the 18th century. It should not be misinterpreted: it is not a history book, it is not particularly accurate in its depictions of Acadian life, nor is it not based on specific events. Despite the fact that her statue can be seen in Grand Pré, Nova Scotia and in Saint Martinville, Louisiana, Evangeline never existed, although both she and Gabriel have been linked to actual historical figures, particularly in Louisiana.

Before Longfellow's poem, however, Katharine Reid Williams had published a novel portraying Acadian life during and after the tragedy of 1755 with the title *The Neutral French*. In many ways this 1841 novel is a more accurate depiction of events than Longfellow's romantic narrative.

One of the Maritime's most famous English-speaking writers, Charles G.D. Roberts, has picked up the story of *Yvonne de Lamourie, a sister to Evangeline*, another story of Grand Pré before and after the Expulsion, blended with a love story.

Numerous other writers have gone the same route. Recreating the old Acadie and extolling the virtues of its inhabitants, was more appealing than trying to understand modern-day Acadians. Marion Davison and Audrey Marsh have given us *Smoke over Grand Pré* in 1983, Robert E. Wall has written *The Acadians* in 1984, Sten Eirik has created a *Geline of Acadia* for younger readers in 1990.

Among the fascinating periods of Acadian history in the 18th century, the story of Charles de la Tour and particularly of his wife has been a major inspiration for some English-speaking writers.

Historians have certainly shown an interest in Acadian history, although a lot of material published in English prior to 1950 should be read with great caution: Acadian history today has brought to light many new facts that were usually ignored in favor of an "idyllic" vision of Acadians as victims—or, in a few cases, as rascals—that was essentially a rewrite of early French writers, like l'abbé Raynal who inspired Haliburton, themselves usually not very accurate. Among the best studies on 18th century Acadie in English we can count the books by Naomi Griffiths, who is respected as a pioneer by Acadian historians themselves.

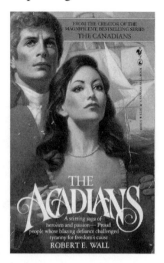

Modern-day Acadie has been far less covered in English than the old Acadie. There are, however, some important books that are easily available. Melvin Gallant's book on Acadians throughout the Maritimes has been translated as *The Country of Acadia*. The first study done by the Acadian Studies Centre at the université de Moncton has been translated as *The Acadians of the Maritimes*. Sally Ross and Alphonse Deveau have produced their book on *The Acadians of Nova Scotia* in English, and the book *The Rise of the French in New Brunswick* can give readers a feel of political and social developments in the Acadian community over the last 25 years.

A number of books show aspects of Acadian reality in various regions and at various times. *Candyman* by Simone Poirier-Bures depicted life among Acadians in Halifax in the 1960s. *I'll Buy You an Ox* by Betty Boudreau Vaughan offers insights into life among the poor of Baie Sainte-Marie during the same period. *My Acadian Heritage* by Léonie Poirier gives a fair idea of some customs in Baie Sainte-Marie in the 1930s and 40s. Similar books, often translated into English, exist for most Acadian regions of the Maritimes. Some will add visual arts and even music to the narrative, such as Catherine Poirier's *Going Home Song* by Dorothy Harley Eber.

Genealogy, in book form or on the Web, is a favorite pastime of Acadians. The Girouard family and related links has been studied in great detail by William H. Gerrior of Halifax in his book *Awakenings,*

MARTINE JACQUOT

L-R: Former publisher Michel Henry and authors Régis Brun, Gérald Leblanc and Herménégilde Chiasson.

---

but a lot of families have a genealogy book devoted to them, sometimes available in English translation or in a bilingual version. The actual fact that most descendants of Acadians today cannot speak or read French, particularly in the United States, makes the availability of such material in English even more important.

VII.   Visual Arts and Film making

Few artifacts of old French Acadie survive today. One of the most notable is in the church at Johnstown, Cape Breton. It is a painting of Christ, which came from the church at Port-Toulouse. The Mi'kmaq kept it intact after the French left, and we can still see it today. Much of the visual art in Acadie before 1755 was connected with churches and chapels, as was true in most of the Western world.

Claude Roussel, pupil of Pio-Carmel Laporte of Edmundston, is considered the first modern Acadian sculptor. Also a painter, he founded the visual arts program at Université de Moncton. His bas reliefs may be seen in the church at Grand Pré, at the city hall of Saint John and on the campus of Université de Moncton. Marie-Hélène Allain, of Sainte-Marie de Kent, is famous for her stone sculptures which can be seen in front of the Beaverbrook Gallery in Fredericton, on the campus of the University of Moncton, and around the world.

Claude Picard, from Saint-Basile, one of the first Acadian visual artists to make a living solely through reliance on his art work was selected to paint scenes in the church at Grand Pré. Nelson Surette is a major Nova Scotia painter of Acadian descent, and Ronald Landry ("Ronald à Gonzague") was one of the many dedicated artists on Ile Madame in Cape Breton: a provincial award now honors his name, kept alive by the use of his art work on ceramics by productions Picasse on Isle Madame. Leo Leblanc painted the Cocagne area. Roméo Savoie is an architect, painter and poet. Painters are often connected to teaching institutions. Hilda Lavoie, an engraver who manages a crafts centre in Nigadoo, also teaches at Collège Communautaire in Dieppe. Painter Claude Gauvin taught in Quebec and the United States before teaching at Université de Moncton and has been in the forefront of art instruction in New Brunswick. Claude Thériault, a painter, works for publishers and teaches and has been president of CARFAC, the national Canadian visual artists' organization. Among the younger generation, Yvon Gallant, Herménégilde Chiasson, Georges Goguen, Paul Bourque, C. Cormier, Nérée de Grâce and sister Eulalie Boudreau are worth mentioning. Daniel Dugas and Paul J. Bourque, among others, are connected with the Galerie Sans Nom in Moncton, the only artist-run centre working in French in the Maritimes, and one of the main sources of inspiration for modern and contemporary forms of art.

Photography and film are ways to preserve reality with a relatively unadulterated eye, and both forms of art are now commonly practised by Acadians. Dolorès Breau and Corinne Gallant have become well-known and helped to preserve images of Acadie and Acadians. François Gaudet has picked up photography from his father, creating increasingly original works and forming new photographers in Nova Scotia. Writers can be photographers too: *Le Pays d'Acadie*, by Melvin Gallant, gives a broad view of several Acadian regions as they are today and is rivalled only by Roméo Cormier's *Images de l'Acadie*, a slide-show as well as a book.

Acadian film is, of course, more recent that Acadian literature. Léonard Forest, a filmmaker from Bouctouche, was a pioneer in both in the 1950s. Some Quebec filmmakers had documented Acadie in the past—the movie *Acadie, Acadie* by Pierre Perrault was a witness to the social turmoil of the late 1960s. Acadian filmmakers received awards each year at the Atlantic Film Festival held in Halifax until 1997. Following the lead of Léonard Forest, filmmakers Phil Comeau,

Herménégilde Chiasson and Anna Girouard provide Acadians with a vision of themselves through their own eyes.

Experience in TV has been helpful for Marc Paulin and Herménégilde Chiasson. Chiasson's film about the Robichaud years and the beginnings of Acadian literature in southeastern New Brunswick, uses excerpts from newsreels of the 1960s to create a sense of continuity in the development of the Acadian community. With *Les Années Noires* and *Epopée*, Herménégilde Chiasson has given a voice to Acadians on their own history. In *In Search of Evangeline* Ginette Pellerin analyzes an Acadian myth as a twentieth century Acadian, looking at the influence of Evangeline on Acadian society. In *The Acadian Connection*, Monique LeBlanc gives us a view of an important connection between all people of Leblanc (or White) lineage in North America. Young women like Renée Blanchar are as active in filmmaking as are actresses like Marie Comeau (who played a part in *The Scarlet Letter*, a movie shot in the Acadian region of the Baie Sainte-Marie area.) Films by Claudette Lajoie-Chiasson, set in the Acadian peninsula, portray the difficulties experienced by women, and working women in particular. Anne-Marie Sirois, also an author of children's books, has done some animated films.

Developments in the 1980s enabled young Acadian filmmakers to enjoy more freedom to create regionally, although the administration of the National Film Board is still concentrated in Montreal. Some francophones who were originally non-Acadian, such as French TV journalist Eric Michel, have been key players in the development of film and filmmakers in Acadie. Diane Poitras, from Montreal, is now in charge of the Office National du Film (ONF) production branch in Moncton. Phil Comeau, to whom we owe *J'avions 375 ans*, has produced the first full-length feature film in Acadie, around the well-known story of Jérôme, the mysterious mute stranger of Baie Sainte-Marie. *Le Secret de Jérôme* has been celebrated in many festivals, from Namur in Belgium to Louisiana. Acadian film is alive and well and, when compared to other regions of the francophone world, worthy of interest in many ways.

One interesting new dimension of Acadian visual expression has been the development of poster art since the 1960s. As young writer and visual artist, Gérald Giroux wrote, "for the artist, the poster became the means by which to recapture his cultural space, dominated by English." Rejecting old symbols by making fun of them and showing how little they were connected with modern Acadian reality enabled graphic artists such as Raymond Thériault and Jean-François Marcil to earn a living and better their craft. The poster, in the words

Filmmaker Phil Comeau.

---

of Giroux, "has become an integral part of the Acadian cultural and artistic industry. It has facilitated the development of an Acadian popular art that wishes to be in accord with the American view of its cultural milieu."

VIII. Handcrafts

Acadians knew how to construct houses, make furniture and build ships. In olden times everything was handmade, but now handcrafted items are a luxury and a lure for cultural tourism. Chéticamp has been renowned for its hooked rugs, a blend of art and industry largely based on women's abilities, since 1923. Elizabeth Lefort has works in the Vatican, the White House and Buckingham Palace, and since 1983 in an art gallery in Chéticamp, where her works are displayed. Baie Sainte-Marie women are renowned for their quilts (couvertures piquées), Handcraft clubs at Grand-Digue and Saint-Paul have exploited themes from *La Sagouine*, and Caraquet has had a co-op handicraft centre since 1965. The work of Les Productions Picasse, on Isle Madame, is a good example of a blend of art and handcrafts. Everywhere, at a time when cultural tourism is on the rise, with support from the industry and governments, there is a drive to have more unique Acadian products for sale.

IX. Festivals

Festivals are a good way to promote culture, and are occasions when communities can feel closer than during the routine of daily chores. In Acadian communities, festivals are also a way to remember a time when communities were tighter-knit than today, when people had to meet to help one another, be it for building a house, thrashing the flax or celebrating a baptism.

Names of festivals are often connected to a particular Acadian reality: Saint-Antoine, New Brunswick, has a Festival de la Poutine, celebrating that typically Acadian meal. Chéticamp, Nova Scotia, has a Festival de l'Escaouette, related to the song and dance by the same name, l'Escaouette. Some Acadian regions, such as Pomquet in Nova Scotia, have winter carnivals, but festivals usually celebrate the gorgeous days of summer and are an important means of attracting tourist dollars and promoting local culture. Celebrations can be on a larger scale: the celebrations for the 375th anniversary of the founding of Port-Royal marked an Acadian renaissance for Nova Scotia, and Acadians can share in many. The 200th anniversary of New Brunswick, and the activities for the 100th anniversary of the first Convention Nationale in 1990, the "Retrouvailles" in 1994, and the planned festivities already discussed for 2004, which may be both the 400th anniversary of the founding of l'Acadie and the third Congrès Mondial, are other major celebrations, past and future.

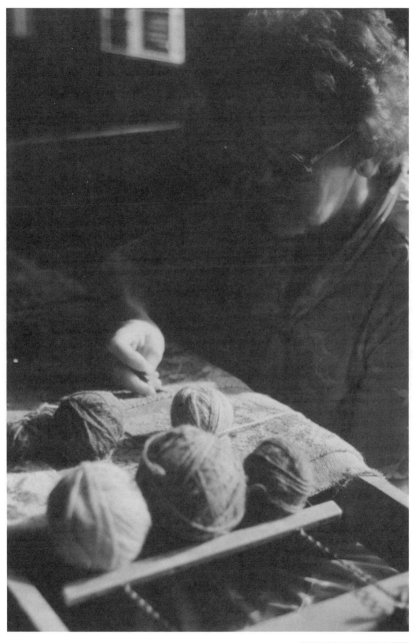

Hooking rugs at Chéticamp.

Moncton has had for years *le frolic*, a festival of song, music and dance. Other places talk about pistrolis. Whatever the name, Acadians love festivals, dances and gatherings, an integral part of their culture. In Caraquet, the Acadian festival lasts three months. Other festivals have broadened their "francophone" meaning, reinforcing linguistic pride. Foire Brayonne in Edmundston combines industrial and cultural interests and is one of the largest festivals of its kind. Around Grand Pré, the Acadian Days festival is now a major annual event. Acadians also take part in Festival-Sur-Mer in Saint John.

The annual blessing of the fishing fleet, in Caraquet.

The traditional and religious reasons for the festivals in Acadian regions vary. One of the most important religious festivals was the *Fête-Dieu*, usually in May, in which whole communities walked around villages, praying the *Saint Sacrement* while little girls threw fresh flower petals in the path of the procession. Anglophone Maritimers often call this festival the French Feast. Many other festivals, usually connected with religion take place from Christmas to Easter. The origin of some festivals predates Christianity. For instance, *La Chandeleur* (Candlemas), on February 2nd, is an occasion to rejoice in the heart of winter. In Chéticamp and in Acadian regions of Prince Edward Island, on La Chandeleur ceremonies took disguised revellers from home to home, collecting food for a party.

During *Mi-Carême*, revellers in disguise dance and rejoice in the middle of Lent. Even those who know little of Acadian folklore known Mardi Gras, which gave New Orleans its major festival and has now been revived for Haligonians of all cultures.

Many festivals were regional in nature and were often linked to the seasons. In Memramcook the *Fête des Petits Oiseaux* (Festival of Little Birds) was celebrated until the mid-twentieth century, to indicate the revival of spring and the new seeds that signified fertility for Acadian cultures. *Fête des Neiges* (Snow Festival) was a day during which priests asked parishioners to pray for good harvests in the year to come. During the periods known as *rogations* in May, or the date of St. Mark's festival, April 25th, priests would bless seeds used for planting. These customs are still followed in Edmundston, where farm and forestry products are brought from all Acadian regions to be blessed at a mass organized for the occasion.

Some Acadian customs are borrowed from other cultures: Halloween, a festival of Celtic origin, was absorbed from the anglophone tradition. Elements of the song of l'Escaouette show that parts of it were borrowed from the Mi'kmaq. But, on the whole, festivities in Acadian regions are largely unique. The major collective celebration of the 15th of August, *Fête Nationale des Acadiens*, only reinforces the obvious: Acadians are a people with their own identity and their own reasons to celebrate what is unique to them.

X. Food and Cuisine

Every community and region on earth finds a way to accommodate the resources nature gave it and develops unique food traditions. This is the case with Acadians as well, and it is therefore not surprising to discover that Acadian cuisine, except in the Madawaska region, has been largely influenced by the sea. In its most simple form, Acadian cuisine was at one time, as poet Louis Comeau remembered from his childhood near Beresford in the 1950s, *des patates pis des harengs*, potatoes and herrings. Until the 1940s, Acadians used simple foods to prepare meals: herring, corn, potatoes, salt bacon and foods made from locally grown grains. They made their own bread, pancakes and tarts. In Madawaska the *ploye*, a buckwheat pancake, became a common part of local meals.

A *fricot*, or boullion, was made of ingredients boiled in a soup that could vary considerably according to region, and made a hearty meal. In northeastern New Brunswick it was made of potatoes and meat, with the addition of *grands-pères* (white pasta) cooked with it.

The meat came from domestic animals such as beef or chicken or from animals hunted such as rabbits or several kinds of birds such as the *petits-noirs* well-liked in Lamèque, or partridges or barnacle geese. In other regions a *fricot*, sometimes called *tchaude* (like a chowder) as in the Magdalen Islands or Chéticamp, would include fish. *Boullion au maquereau* (mackerel soup) was particularly appreciated in Caraquet. Now also sold in cans at supermarkets around the Maritimes, the *fricot* is probably the best known and one of the most delicious examples of Acadian cuisine.

Before the Expulsion, Acadian farms were large, and what we known now leads us to believe that all the vegetables found in France were also found in Acadie. Farmers raised their own cattle but relied on hogs for most of their meat and lard. Cows provided milk, butter and cream. Oxen were generally used for farm work, as horses were few. Sheep provided wool. A few geese (called *pirounes* in Acadian French) and hens and chickens were also to be found on farms.

After 1713, Acadians farmed lands of poorer quality than the original lands around Port-Royal, and the choice of vegetables became more limited. Turnips (called *nave* or *naveau*) and cabbage were resistant to frost, and the settlers also added beans, corn and that fundamental ingredient of Acadian cuisine, potatoes. Acadians had apple trees and grew several kinds of grain. They also found the small berries nature provided, *les grainages*—strawberries, blueberries, gooseberries (*les pommes de pré*), blackberries and many others. They learned to grow or use several natural herbs and spices, from caraway seeds (*anis*) to coriander and savoury. Several plants such as mint (*baume*), sarsaparilla and plantain were used for medicinal purposes as well. Dandelions could be eaten in a salad, as could wild spinach. By 1700 the virtues of maple syrup had been discovered by Acadian farmers, who could get other forms of sugar only through trade. Needless to say, maple syrup was the most sought after attraction at the Poitiers trade fair where Acadians were celebrated in 1993.

Most of these features were kept throughout the nineteenth century, when fish, until then a secondary source of food, were increasingly eaten. For a long time, it was herring and cod. Little by little, other kinds were added—gaspereau, Boston bluefish, smelt, trout. In many regions, seafood became an essential part of Acadian cuisine—clams, oysters, lobster. Lobster fishing, for which Acadian fishermen came to be known the world over, only became commercial on a large scale at the end of the nineteenth century. Crab fishing, which led to new dishes, started in the 1960s on the Acadian peninsula.

Potatoes can be used in many ways. In New Brunswick, one of

the most common forms was to make *poutines*, particularly *poutine rôpée*, made with grated potatoes cooked in the *fricot* and usually with a centre of meat or fish. In Nova Scotia, *rappie pie* or *rôpure*, was made. The *pot-en-pot* (another kind of stew) could replace the fricot. Vegetables were used for soups; marsh plants added a unique flavour with poetic names like *passe-pierre* or *tétine de souris*. When only potatoes were available, the *fricot* became a poor person's meal, *a fricot à la belette*, without meat or fish.

Pork, beef and chicken are found in traditional Acadian dishes, as are wild meats, such as rabbit and porcupine. Desserts were sometimes made from poutines made with dough, sugar and raisins, such as *poutine à trou* or *pets de soeur* (nun's farts), biscuits mixed with molasses and cinnamon. Tarts made with fat from seals as on the Magdalen Islands and buckwheat pancakes called *ployes* in the Madawaska region of New Brunswick, could either be dessert or a meal.

Acadian dishes are a tribute to the inventiveness of a people who made the best possible use of the natural resources available to them. Traditional Acadian life followed the rhythm of the seasons: fish, eggs and milk were the food of summer, when meat was uncommon; fresh vegetables and berries were available after July; poultry could be eaten while waiting for the season of real meat, when animals would be killed in November, to provide food for the wintertime. Salt or dried fish, bread, lard and molasses provided important sources of nourishment. Coffee was uncommon, tea was rarely found, and beer was often made from spruce or grain, the *flacatoune* so well-liked by Antonine Maillet's characters.

Special celebrations called for special meals. For Christmas and the festival period leading up to the New Year, most Acadians ate roast goose, rabbit pie and *galettes* (tarts) and poutines for dessert. Some children would receive *naulets*, biscuits in the shape of particular characters. For the Epiphany, Twelfth Night, a cake was made with buttons inside, or a pea and a bean, to select the king and queen of the evening—a tradition present throughout Western francophone countries. Candlemas was pancake night, and every one of the guests had to turn his or her own pancake—not succeeding in doing so might be a forerunner of trouble. Easter offered a meal of eggs, followed by bacon or ham at lunchtime, an omelette or pastry with maple syrup in the evening. For special occasions such as weddings, as many dishes as possible were provided, and on some special occasions all the people in a community, especially women, would assemble to prepare meals for a huge picnic.

Although modern times changed what people ate, Acadian dishes are still largely based on traditional sources of food and are part of a broader Maritime heritage. New francophones have brought to the Maritimes a more European type of cuisine. French or Swiss chefs such as Georges Frachon of La Fine Grobe in Nigadoo, New Brunswick and Alex Clavel of Chez La Vigne in Wolfville, Nova Scotia, did much to develop standards for the restaurant business, showing inventiveness in the blend of modern and traditional foods from their new and former countries. Acadians are also learning a greater variety of meals from their southern cousins in Louisiana (with more spices and different meats and shellfish) and other, more exotic forms of cuisine from, for example, Haiti or North Africa.

XI. Science and Research

Acadian farmers acted as the first "civil engineers" in the Maritimes when they reclaimed land from the sea on a large scale. They knew how to build dykes that withstood the test of time and allowed the production of grain and other crops on fertile lands. These lands were initially around the Bay of Fundy, but gradually, the system of aboiteaux was extended to all Acadian regions, even along the coasts of the Gaspé. These sturdy constructions required a collective effort to be built and maintained, and were rarely damaged except by huge storm tides or accumulations of ice. Many of the dykes today have the appearance of natural barriers, and the total amount of land recovered by these early engineers amounts to roughly 750,000 acres or 1,172 square miles—the equivalent to about half the surface of Prince Edward Island. Often, however, the old Acadian dykes are hard to find today, having been washed out by the sea; the Planters, Loyalists, and other settlers usually used Acadian techniques to build more modern wood or stone dykes behind the original aboiteaus.

Even as farmers along the Bay of Fundy, Acadian knew better ways to dry, salt and cure fish than did most employees of French companies. As fishermen, they honed their skills to greater perfection. It is not surprising that Caraquet, with only about 4,000 inhabitants, has today the only fisheries school in New Brunswick. Today factories where fish or crab are processed are increasingly modern, and fishermen's unions have to worry about which type of fish to catch and what quota systems they should agree to. Modern fishing calls for clear technical skills and knowledge. However, fishing is still a family tradition. For example, mussel producer Cécile Lanteigne of Caraquet is the daughter and granddaughter of fishermen, and her work calls for knowledge closely connected to work done at the

Bedford Institute of Oceanography in Nova Scotia on cultivated mussels, as well as hard labour!

Forestry is an important element in Acadian life, although most of the pulp and paper companies operating in Acadian regions are branches of American companies. The creation of a forestry program at Université de Moncton, approved for the Edmundston campus in the 1980s, was important for the development of specialists in that field. Here again, Acadians had developed their skills in many ways without formal education. Until 1713, they had furnished the French

MARTINE JACQUOT

Boats in the harbour at Caraquet, New Brunswick.

navy with pine masts. They knew how to use water as a power source (they had built mills as early as the time of Port-Royal), and in the Clare district, for instance, two sawmills existed in 1785. Gradually, as business opportunities grew, more were built, and particularly after 1870 they became technically better and more efficient. In the flatlands of Louisiana, they devised ways to use pack animals as a power source.

Wood was used to build boats and (contrary to the strange notion that Acadians had no part in the golden age of sail in the Maritimes) some regions were heavily involved in boatbuilding. Sawing wood and working as carpenters for others, Acadians of Clare, for instance gradually became master carpenters, then boatbuilders and ship-owners. Between 1900 and 1920 many boats were built, until the age of sail ended a few years later. Master carpenters from the Baie, such as Antoine Deveau, Uriel Leblanc or Théophile Leblanc, had no choice but to leave for the United States. Boatbuilding remains a major industry: at La Butte (Meteghan River) boatbuilders A.F. Thériault and sons employ up to 150 workers and have built more than 170 trawlers. When Université Sainte-Anne introduced a course in boatbuilding, they recognized a skill with an Acadian tradition, although such courses are more often found at the level of colleges.

At a more formal level, Acadians at centres today work on applied research such as electronic advances for small business and new technologies, for example at CADMI (Centre for the Application and Development of Incorporated Microelectronics) at Université de Moncton. In 1989, French Canadian scientists and researchers in the ACFAS (French Canadian Association for the Advancement of Sciences) met at Université de Moncton. Francophone researchers working in English-speaking institutions sometimes feel cut off from their own cultural base. However, with the progress of new technologies, better information and better translation facilities, the time when research in several fields could only be conducted in English is past, and conferences such as this indicate that French is also a language of research in the Maritimes.

XII. Sports

In sports as everywhere else, better coordination has improved the visibility of Acadian athletes. Schools and universities play a large part in their development. Every year all Acadian regions take part in Jeux de l'Acadie, an organization managed by Acadians from all regions of New Brunswick, and representatives from Nova Scotia and Prince Edward Island. In 1990 the finals took place on Prince Edward Island, in the Evangéline region, the only Acadian region on the island; in 1998 they were held at Moncton, New Brunswick. Support by school systems and Acadian financial institutions such as the *caisses populaires* (credit unions) and Compagnie l'Assomption, a large insurance company, make Jeux de l'Acadie an important component in Acadian sports development. Acadian athletes can go beyond the national level, as Canada regularly takes part in Jeux de la francophonie, the francophone equivalent of the Commonwealth games.

Joël Bourgeois is one of the important track and field athletes in

Acadian sports, having taken part in the Atlanta Olympics in 1996. Although Acadians have produced no Olympic champions, they most certainly have produced a good number of important figures in sports considering the small size of the Acadian community at the international level. The best-known sports personality of Acadian descent is no doubt the former captain of the Montreal Canadiens, Jean Belliveau, winner of a number of Stanley Cups and one of the great players in the history of hockey. Although born in Quebec, Jean Belliveau still considers himself proud of his Acadian origins.

Acadians would not be Canadians if they did not share the common passion of anglophones and francophones alike for hockey. The best symbol of Acadian success in this may be the hockey team at Université de Moncton, les Aigles Bleus (Blue Eagles). A team usually made up of a mix of Acadian and Québécois players, and attracting major coaches such as Jean Perron, it won another Canadian championship in 1989. Hockey is only one of the sports in which one can find Acadian athletes, and many activities take place at Université de Moncton, from soccer to volleyball and baseball, for men and women alike. All regions of Acadie have hockey teams that are now getting increasingly recognized, from the Matadors of Mathieu Martin to the Titan in Acadie-Bathurst, which is now a team of the powerful Junior Hockey League of Quebec (the LHJMQ). Another team in the Acadian peninsula is now part of the Atlantic league. Campbellton has its skating temple of fame, honoring figure skaters as well as former hockey players, like Claude "Buck" Cyr, who played with the Campbellton Tigers.

Sometimes, Acadian hockey players will reach the coveted status of NHL player: this is the case of Réal Daigle, who played with the Ottawa Senators, and of Scott Pellerin, from Shediac, who is now playing with the St. Louis Blues.

Acadians, as evidenced by the Jeux de l'Acadie, play all kinds of sports, women as well as men. This is probably one of the reasons to hope that the Canada Winter Games of 2003 might take place in the Acadian peninsula. Softball, baseball, and now soccer are among the sports that see Acadian teams in good positions nationally in their respective leagues. Here again, some players will gradually emerge to go beyond regional fame. The name of Eric Lebreton is often mentioned these days in senior volleyball; and Rhéal Cormier became a major league player in baseball, with the Cardinals in St. Louis. Young Suzanne Gerrior, a Halifax girl of Acadian descent, obtained scholarships from US universities on the strength of her soccer play, and was part of the Canadian national soccer team. Acadians have also made their mark in sports for handicaped people: Edmundston hosted the special Winter Olympics, and a player like Mike Doucet is making himself known in basketball for wheelchair athletes at an international level.

Individual sports are also an important part of the Acadian sports landscape. Not all boxers reach the fame of Yvon Durelle, the boxer from Baie Sainte-Anne known as the fighting fisherman, who was the most prominent name in sports of his day. Born in 1929 of Basque-Acadian ancestry, the son of a local blacksmith and a strong-willed Robichaud mother, he won many matches in the Maritimes and the United States from 1947 to 1963. Durelle became Canadian middleweight champion, and then light heavyweight champion a few months later, a title lost but recaptured in 1955. Commonwealth champion of light heavyweights in 1957, he never succeeded in becoming world champion but left boxing as a tough and very strong fighter.

It is widely rumored these days that Nora Daigle, a female boxer from Southeastern New Brunswick, has a good shot at an international boxing crown. France Gagné, in Edmundston, brought to her community four national Canadian championships in rhythmic gymnastics for women, won by her students. Lise Gautreau was one of the gymnasts who was at the Seoul Olympics, representing Canada. Joël Bourgeois of New Brunswick has taken part in the Atlanta Olympics in track and field. Terry Bastarache and Sheldon Atkinson are both Acadians with a bright future in karaté, a sport that is widely practiced in New Brunswick's Acadian regions.

For a small community these are important achievements, sometimes reinforced by the presence in Acadie of other athletes, like African boxer Greg Tadzi who lived in Moncton for a few years.

Any visitor to Acadian regions knows that Acadians, like other Maritimers, are avid golfers. All Acadian regions have golf courses, and playing golf, at whichever level, is often an important bridge between communities. Sometimes again, a better golfer appears, like young Yannick Lang, from Beresford, who is now at the Club de Golf Royal in Montreal, and hopes to reach national prominence as a player in the next few years.

Golf is not the only exhibition sports Acadians practice or watch. The town of Cocagne is well-known for its international regattas, one of the important speed-boat shows in North America. Quebec and New Brunswick have created a snowmobile race in the wintertime called "Challenge Acadie". The region of Cheticamp in Cape Breton has been in the forefront of cycling tours as well as nature walks. Canoe trips across Nova Scotia do not frighten canoeists from the

Baie Sainte-Marie, as they gather annually around Easter. Cross-country skiing is, in Acadie as well as in the whole Maritimes, an important way to keep in shape in winter. And, to promote physical fitness, Acadian communities like Caraquet take part annually in friendly challenges against communities from around the world. Sports, often forgotten by those who analyze Acadian society, is an important symbol of the vitality and diversity of the Acadian community in the Maritimes.

XIII. Business

Before 1755, the majority of Acadians were farmers, although some, following in the footsteps of Nicolas Denys, discovered how to make a fortune and formed a small "elite" of wealthy merchants, which included the tycoon Joseph-Nicolas Gaultier (1689-1752), known as "Bellair," who suffered cruelly at the hands of the British, and Joseph LeBlanc (1697-1772), known as "Le Maigre," who ended his life at Belle-Ile-en-Mer in Brittany. Although the limited view that English is the language of business stuck longer in Canada (and even in the minds of French Canadians) than anywhere in the world, Acadians had proven that they could easily be successful business people.

In fact, business was sometimes more important to some than their attachment to the Acadian community. Louis Robichaux is a good example of this kind of attitude. A merchant born at Annapolis Royal in 1704, Robichaux was one of the few Acadians in favour of the British regime, and he did not hesitate to take the oath of fidelity to King George III in 1729. He did everything he could to help the English during the period that followed 1744, was taken prisoner by the French and escaped twice, but could not escape being deported like all other Acadians! He had one privilege, though: he was able to choose where to go, and decided to go to New England, where he lived for eleven years, in Boston and Cambridge, before coming back to Quebec in 1755, where he died. He is the father of Vénérande Robichaux, one of the first chroniclers of Acadian life, and an ancestor to the founders of Meteghan.

All countries live off money loaned, earned and spent, but Acadians who came back after the Deportation, or came out of hiding or prisons camps, had little. They had their lands, their courage and a desire to settle land, not so much to produce food for sale, but just to have enough to live on. Afterwards they strove to purchase land of their own. The end of the nineteenth century, in particular, was an intense period of "colonization" which the clergy felt would keep

Acadians on the land and discourage their leaving for the New England manufacturing centres. The Memramcook and Madawaska regions were chosen for this purpose. The Acadian population in the Maritimes increased after 1860 as people went to Saint-Alexis de Matapédia, and to Saint-Paul and Adamsville in Kent County.

In France, Rameau de Saint-Père collected money to help "the cause." Father Louis Gagnon left Shippagan in 1872 to found the Saint-Isidore parish. Father François-Marcel Richard founded Rogersville, Acadieville and more villages in the Kent County area, that were largely the result of the construction of the CNR railway that was supposed to help Acadians. Monsignor Arthur Melanson, Vicar of Campbellton, looked after the colonies between Campbellton and Saint-Léonard in Madawaska County. He even wrote books to entice Acadians to return to the land. A bank for this and a bank for that was the way to get the farmers organized. Credit unions and study groups were introduced. In Saint-Louis de Kent an oats bank lasted for thirty-eight years. In the Richibouctou area it was an egg club, a kind of co-op to sell eggs. In 1929 there were fifty of these clubs in New Brunswick. The settlers remained poor, but they were often self-sufficient until modern times, when many gave up farming to seek employment in the cities.

The image of Acadians is associated with the sea. Most Acadians had to spread along the coast and became fishermen, farming the land, if any, for their own use. Foreign companies, especially from Jersey, exploited the Acadians as much as they could while buying their fish. With the arrival of the co-operative movement, however, Acadians achieved a certain economic freedom. In 1907 a group of miners from Sydney Mines, Cape Breton, organized a store; in 1915, fishermen from Chéticamp established a fishing co-op; and the first Acadian credit union was founded in 1916 in Richibouctou-Village. In New Brunswick the co-operative movement boomed among Acadians because it corresponded with the community-type government they had always known as part of their culture. In 1985 Acadian credit unions (*caisses populaires*) had assets of $485 million and 180,000 shareholders. The Fédération des Caisses Populaires in Caraquet is a major Acadian institution, although its relative wealth today should not mislead observers in understanding how difficult it was for the generation of people like Martin Légère in the 1940s, to build Acadian financial institutions.

The co-operative movement, from the 1930s, particularly, has helped to ensure that Acadian fishermen received their fair share of profits, but private enterprises were also developed by Acadians.

Businessman Bernardin Comeau of Baie Sainte-Marie.

Comeau Seafoods, managed by Bernardin Comeau, is one of many Acadian enterprises that provide employment and a trading contact with the world.

Today Acadians are responsible for 100 per cent of the crab production in New Brunswick, presently worth about $66 million a year, 100 per cent of the shrimp production, worth $14 million annually, and 100 per cent of the Boston bluefish production, a $2.5 million industry. Acadian fishermen bring in 84 per cent of the cod fished by New Brunswickers—$11 million out of a provincial total of $13 million! Lobsters harvested by Acadian regions in the Maritimes in 1982 provided the basis of a $20 million industry. Since the 1960s, Acadians, with the help of the co-operative movement, some private enterprises, their own expertise and business stamina, unionization, and the support of federal and provincial fisheries ministers often coming from Acadian regions, have fought against foreign monopolies, developed new fisheries and products and made fishing synonymous with their community as a whole. Even though fishing is now in a crisis, new ways to grow fish in fish tanks are being explored in many colleges and schools.

Lobster fishing aided the development of Acadian communities during the second half of the nineteenth century. With the opening of lobster pounds, *homarderies*, like that of Freeman Kimball at Bas-Cap Pelé in 1874, fishing communities developed quickly, moving from a subsistence economy to the pre-industrial age. Bas-Cap-Pelé benefited enormously from such developments: stores, hotels, hardware retailers, and photography studios were able to open for business.

In these lobster enterprises, Acadians often played subservient roles as foremen to anglophone bosses, but some were able to manage their own businesses, such as Dominique Léger of Westmoreland County, New Brunswick (1855-1928). In 1891, people such as Léger, Anselme Petitpas, Siméon Hébert, François Doiron and others owned firms that packaged lobster for the British market and other consumers. Male and female employees often worked for only $6.00 per month, earning barely enough to reimburse what they had bought on credit the previous winter, sometimes from a manager-owned store. However, these businesses provided employment and enabled Acadians to stay home instead of leave to find work.

Historians such as Régis Brun have started to study the essential industry that lobster fishing has been for Acadians throughout the Maritimes since the middle of the nineteenth century. In southwestern Nova Scotia, for instance, in Par en Bas (the villages of Yarmouth County) family businesses thrived with names such as d'Eon, d'Entremont or Amiro.

During the 1980s Acadian businesses were growing. Universities aided development through direct spending and salaries, by shaping managers and skilled workers of tomorrow, tremendously broadened the potential development of Acadian businesses. Léopold Belliveau, ex-mayor of Moncton, feels that the real economic power of Acadians in New Brunswick (about 35 per cent of the population) far exceeds their numbers. Acadians have understood that control over their economy is the only way to control their destiny as a community.

Société l'Assomption is a good example of this. Acadians had had a long tradition of helping each other out when times became difficult, and at the beginning of the twentieth century the idea grew that some fraternal organization would bring together all Acadians, including those forced to leave their Maritime homeland to find employment in American cities. On August 16, 1902, at the National Congress, Lucien Belliveau suggested that all Acadian groups organize a fraternal organization and a school fund. On May 30, 1903, the project was under way, and on September 8th, the first constitution of La Société l'Assomption was adopted. Its aims were to gather all Acadians under the same flag, assist the sick, to help financially the heirs of deceased members, and to maintain and improve language, culture and religion. A school fund was set aside, and in 1904 the society was extended to the three Maritime provinces. In 1913 the head office was transferred to Moncton. In 1969 it became solely a mutual insurance company. And today it is a major financial institution in the Maritimes. Place l'Assomption, the highest building in Moncton, has become a source of pride for Acadians in a city where their rights were for a long time ignored or rejected.

Acadian businesses have been growing, regrouping, and learning new managerial skills over the past twenty years. Atlantic Compressed Air, the Da Vinci software company in Edmundston, Optique Océan in Moncton, Imperial Sheet Metal in Richibuctou, Les Produits de la Mer in le Goulet, les Algues Acadiennes in Halifax—all are proof of a new-found strength, also present in provincial economic councils, such as Le Conseil Economique du Nouveau-Brunswick, with its 1,500 members (up from 50 in 1979). A good number of the 4,300 regular students on the three campuses of Université de Moncton will go into business, law or communications, all of which will produce a healthy environment for future business and community development. Research is growing, and products from Acadian regions (such as crab from les Produits de la Mer in Le Goulet, employer of 500 people, and turf exported from Shippagan to the United States or Japan) are likely to be in constant demand. New areas of development lie in tourism, despite a serious lag in tourist infrastructures in most Acadian regions: not only do Acadian organizations try to bridge the gap by a more aggressive presence of Acadians in international tourist trade, but individual businesses also attempt to offer new opportunities; the Bernard Cyr Group is undertaking construction of a hotel for Moncton in 1999, just in time for the francophone summit. How many Maritimers are aware that Pizza Delight was founded by two Acadian graduates from l'Université de Moncton business school?

XIV. Religious Life

The France of Louis XIII has been described as "the eldest daughter of the Catholic Church," and French citizens of Reformed faith were persecuted and hounded at the time Acadie was originally founded. Acadians were, of course, deeply and profoundly Catholic, and they still are. Many movements are based on Catholic institutions, the anointment of a new bishop is a major event and clerics are still part of the Acadian "establishment." In some regions, not going to Mass on Sunday is still viewed in a bad light, especially in smaller villages, and an ingrained distrust of Protestants sometimes remains, although people are now more tolerant than in the early nineteenth century, when Father Sigogne refused to wed a Catholic girl and a Protestant paramour (although such marriages seem to have been common in the 18th century).

In 1850 there were only two priests of Acadian origin in the Maritimes; most of the priests who devoted their lives to the Acadian community were either of French or, more often, of Québécois origin.

Some of the worst fights between Acadians and anglophones at the end of the nineteenth century had to do with the election of an Acadian bishop and the organization of an Acadian parish. Saint-Joseph College helped many Acadians to become priests, but the Scottish and Irish bishops sent them to English-speaking, rather than Acadian parishes. Father Marcel-François Richard went to Rome twice to petition the Pope for an Acadian bishop, Acadians being by far the largest Catholic group in the Maritimes, and Pope Pius X offered a golden chalice as a token of his promise to provide Acadians with a bishop drawn from among them. In 1912, Monsignor Edouard LeBlanc, pastor of Saint-Bernard church in Nova Scotia, was made bishop of Saint John, New Brunswick. Since then, Acadian dioceses have been created and, despite a lingering linguistic problem in some cases, the recognition of Acadians by the Catholic Church has been consistent. Pope John Paul II gave a clear proof of his concern for Acadians when he visited Moncton on his Canadian tour in 1984.

Roman Catholic church at Petite-Rivière-de-l'Ile, near Lamèque, New Brunswick.

XV. The military

Acadians, quite naturally, fought for their land: the famous Battle of Bloody Creek, where they routed British soldiers, is only the best-known example of a popular militia that developed in the 18th century, despite the fact that Acadians were not, by and large, a fighting community. Beausoleil Broussard was the best example of "freedom fighter" of his time.

It would, therefore, have been surprising not to find some Acadians in the military, be it in Canada or in other countries. Before Acadians were involved as soldiers—and, rarely, as officers—in Canada's two world wars, some of them were actively involved in the major American war of the 19th century, the American civil war. Most Cajuns—like most Creole officers—were of course on the side of the Confederacy, defending the South of which Louisiana was part: Cajuns even had their own general, with Alfred Mouton, son of governor and sugar-cane planter Alexandre Mouton. Born at Opelousas in 1829, this brilliant Acadian was killed in action at the age of 35 after leading his militia in battles as important as Pittsburgh Landing and Shiloh. He is the first American military hero of Acadian origin.

There were, however, Acadians on the blue side as well as the gray: Dosithé Porelle, born in 1840 at Saint-André, near Shédiac, enrolled in the New Hampshire Volunteers in 1862. He fought in the famous battles of the Wilderness and Shenandoah Valley, and was wounded several times, last in 1864. Promoted sever-al times for bravery, he was proof again that Acadians are able to be present in mili-tary action as

Dosithé Porelle (centre) fought in the U.S. civil war on the side of the Blue. He is shown here with his mother Appaline Hebert and his brothers.

well as any other Americans or Canadians. He died in 1928.

There were numerous Acadians in the Canadian forces in WWI

and WWII. In fact, the town of Dieppe, near Moncton, is named in memory of the disastrous Canadian Raid on Dieppe, France. One such person was Edgar Cyr, from Edmundston, who joined the Carleton and York regiment in 1941 as a private. Commissioned lieutenant, he left for England in 1943, and then saw war in Italy. Twice wounded by German mortars, he came back to serve Canada as a public servant, while being active in the Legion, where Acadian veterans could share memories with veterans from all other groups in the Maritimes.

Today, Acadian soldiers in Canada's forces are part of Canada's attempts at being more a peacemaker than a warmonger: there are Acadian soldiers in Bosnia, in Cyprus, all around the world, contributing perhaps even better to Canada's peace work because their own people has learned how much war and discrimination can cause long-lasting chaos in a community.

CHAPTER 5

Acadians in the Maritimes in the 1990s

I. Geographic, Linguistic, and Educational Challenges

Acadians have always been consciously North American as well as French. Some analysts, such as Gareau, claim that the Maritimes and New England are parts of a common region. However, the pull on some regions of Acadie, particularly in New Brunswick, is clearly towards the other neighbouring region, Quebec. Language, a common sense of history, and the need to maintain connections with the francophone world clearly indicate this.

Acadie today has to learn how to play on a global scale, taking all the different pulls upon it into account while retaining and developing its collective and many regional differences.

Acadie should not become simply a tourist park, a "Sagouine-land," that will bear witness to a vanished race. It can bring as much to the Maritimes as the anglophone majority can, and it should play a key role in our collective part in the francophone commonwealth. The fact that Acadians and anglophones may at times have diverging interests should not be considered detrimental to our well being—quite to the contrary. It enables us to broaden our views and strengthens the whole maritime region.

Acadians are not going to move to Quebec. They are also not, on a mass scale, going to assimilate into the anglophone majority, although that danger will always be present and may indeed in the long run lower the number of francophones in P.E.I. and Nova Scotia unless measures taken now reverse the trends that became apparent in the 1960s.

Between 1750 and 1800, Acadians had few choices. They were dispersed without their consent, on a scale paralleled to that of the

Blacks or Jews, even if the numbers involved were relatively smaller. After 1850, economic pressures forced many Maritime Acadians to move to New England, other parts of the United States and Canada to earn a living wage, even though this migration often meant leaving behind their Acadian way of life. Those who stayed could not ignore the presence of powerful English-speaking neighbours and of trade links that connected them to Europe and the Caribbean.

MARTINE JACQUOT

Acadian Museum at Abram-Village, P.E.I.

Incredible stories could be written drawing on the oral traditions handed down in Acadian families. These accounts would reflect the history of a specific North American community that is an essential part of our common heritage and one that should not be lost to the world.

Francophones are slowly getting a better share of what they should always have had. Cultural centres, economic projects, political power—these are not alien things anymore. But are they enough? Can Acadie survive without a new collective goal? And how should that take shape? Acadians are still facing, after nearly four centuries, a lot of unanswered questions and many challenges. La francophonie is a beautiful idea for the elite, but for the larger number of Acadians, the first question is: will it help me get a job?

As times changed, so did Acadians. As rural folk with an oral culture, as ordinary and often poor people with a clerical elite, Acadians have had to change quickly in recent decades to adjust to threats posed by the modern world. On an increasingly integrated planet, their communities were small, they had no major political or economic power, and they had a long history of being servants to largely unpleasant and exploitative masters, with little hope (in contrast to the Québécois) of ever having a country of their own to compensate for the sufferings and difficulties of the past. They still have no town that can really be considered a capital for all of them. Moncton is still largely an English-speaking city, although it is increasingly possible to live in French there, and bilingualism, as in Bathurst, is more and more obvious; Caraquet, where little English is heard, is not a very large community.

Every day, Acadians have faced new difficulties. Obtaining rights had always been an uphill battle, sometimes both funny and tragic, as remembered in the movie *L'Acadie, l'Acadie*, about a minimal recognition of the Acadian fact in Moncton in the 1970s. Even in 1985, some members of the anglophone community during hearings on bilingualism in New Brunswick chose to voice their discontent with streams of verbal abuse. The request for French place names on Nova Scotia's French Shore, granted in the 1980s, had led to local brawls ten years earlier. It was still difficult in some instances to be served by NB Tel in French—getting the classic "Sorry, I don't speak French"—in the 1980s. The school debate in Chéticamp in the same years led to bitter infighting between defenders of "bilingual" and of "Acadian" (i.e. primarily francophone) schools. The school debate about a francophone school in Sydney, Nova Scotia, turned into a debate not so much about numbers as about the potentially racist undertones in a school board's attitude. There is still no totally francophone administrative district in the province of New Brunswick. Five French-speaking public libraries in northern New Brunswick depend upon the sole anglophone library in the region. The list could go on. In some cases, as in southwestern Nova Scotia, the fight was between Acadians about the linguistic mix they felt best for their own school system.

Yet the 1980s marked the coming of age of the Acadian community. Even in Nova Scotia—where the number of francophone Acadians seems to dwindle with each national census, largely through "assimilation" into the English-speaking majority, and where few francophones come from outside the province—Acadians now have increased control over their school systems, better opportunities to create their own curricula, a recently created community college, a new institution of higher learning, and their identity clearly recognized in some other institutions. Younger English-speaking Canadians are increasingly more tolerant and more open to French Canadian and Acadian realities than in the past. However, Acadians are still a minority in all three maritime provinces, their present "revival" is still a struggle, and there is no Acadian province or government with powers over, for example, immigration or economic policies.

MARTINE JACQUOT

Les Trois Pignons cultural centre, Chéticamp, N.S.

Acadians are among the more than six million Canadians who speak French, one million of whom live outside Quebec. They know they are a minority on a largely anglophone continent, but six million is a large figure. Switzerland, for example, has fewer inhabitants than that and not more than one million French speakers.

French Canadians feel that they are not just one minority among all the minorities in the multicultural pot, but that they are one of the founding groups of Canada. Even though they were not involved in large numbers in organizing Confederation, they are still part of that group. Most Acadians in fact, are among the 400,000 Canadians who feel that they are "bilingual." Most of them have to be. How can one be "bilingual" without losing one's identity? The answer lies in increased use of what Acadians have won.

There is no comparison between their numbers and those of other minorities in the Maritimes. In New Brunswick there are about 7,000 people of other minorities, compared to 225,000 Acadians and francophones, now increasingly considered truly equal to their anglophone counterparts in that province. Nova Scotia has only 30,000 francophones, but this is still twice the total of all other minorities combined. Prince Edward Island's 5,000 francophones are five times more numerous than all the other minorities together.

Acadians know that, at the federal and the provincial level, attention will be paid to their needs by their own representatives and by others. But how long will the smaller communities survive? How are young people going to adjust to primarily rural regions when cities are more and more attractive? Are a few cultural centres, some activities in French and some schools enough to protect minorities from assimilation? At a time when a majority of Québécois think of political independence from Canada as a realistic option, many Acadians in New Brunswick feel that they may have, sometime in the future, a difficult choice to face.

II. Political Challenges

Political analyst Dalton Camp, in an *Atlantic Insight* column from the 1980s, wondered why Acadians could not have their own province if they wanted to—it would neither alter nor destroy the Maritime or Canadian balance. It could even make some English-speaking diehard defenders of a "unilingual" Canada happy. The Acadian province could, like Quebec, be essentially francophone, and other provinces might be "freed" of providing services in French. Such a province has already been mapped: it would essentially be the northern half of New Brunswick, with a line drawn across the province from Moncton in the south to Edmundston in the northwest. It may look simple, but it is not. Would Nova Scotia or P.E.I. Acadians leave their homes? Probably not. Would all New Brunswick Acadians agree to separate from major cities such as Saint John, in which they are likely to find employment, without the guarantee of similar opportunities in the north? Would Moncton or Chatham anglophones be thrilled to suddenly find themselves members of a minority? Even those who staunchly defended the idea of an Acadian province in the 1970s have come to recognize how hard it may be to think along those lines. Acadians live more in a situation similar to those neighbors of long-standing, the Irish; the core of Acadians is in New Brunswick (like in the Irish Republic), but with an important group in Nova Scotia, P.E.I. and to a smaller extent, in Newfoundland (like the Irish in Ulster); and a very large number is outside the basic territory, primarily in the United States.

But even those who do not like to see the Acadian flag floating today at the New Brunswick-Nova Scotia border or on the legislative building in Fredericton have to admit that French Canada as a whole has more inhabitants than a good number of independent countries (more than Switzerland, Bolivia, Denmark or Finland, for example) and that there are more than twice as many Acadians and francophones in the Maritime provinces than there are inhabitants in Prince Edward Island, which enjoys full provincial status.

Were Acadie to become suddenly, by the touch of a magic wand, an independent country, Acadians would find themselves in a country more populous than Monaco, the Maldives, Iceland, Liechtenstein or San Marino. No wonder that, increasingly, the Acadian reality is recognized by governments in the Maritimes as a "fourth province," even though it is not in one piece and has neither official borders nor status at the table of Confederation.

Some anglophone historians, such as Mason Wade, have noted the marked contrast between the attitudes of the aggressive and sometimes violent Québécois and the peaceful Acadians. This difference is based not so much on nature as on the fact that one group is a majority, long treated as a minority in its own province, that has finally stood up without regard for what others might think, the other is a community without a province of its own that has had to grab little by little whatever it could to make its situation better. Acadians, said Antonine Maillet, have been like the fox, stubborn but sly; yet, when their voices had to be heard, they have been heard.

The measures taken from the 1960s on to enable the Acadian minority in each Maritime province to have better control over its own development and to participate as a partner in provincial and federal advances, have appeared to be late and sometimes too little. And it was difficult to know whether the new directions were aimed at correcting the errors of the past or were simply a federal accommodation of the increased assertiveness in Quebec politics. However, the obvious reality is that Acadians have become more active, present and professional in all fields.

It is also obvious that the fate of Acadians is linked to future negotiations between the federal government and Quebec. Never have the opportunities been greater, but the dangers are also enormous.

III. Inevitable Social Change

The problems of Acadians have differed from those encountered by other groups. Groups that are neither English nor French-speaking in the Maritimes are generally too small to be granted a separate school system or other structures that would recognize their existence as a distinct society, with the exception of the native Mi'kmaq. Being recent immigrants to Canada, except for the Mi'kmaq and Blacks, these groups will, while retaining some specific ethnic traits, blend sooner or later into one of the two main linguistic groups in the Maritimes, probably into the anglophone majority, but in some cases into the francophone minority. Immigrants of French, Haitian, Swiss and Belgian origin will probably feel closer to French Canadian culture in the Maritimes than to Anglo-Canadian culture, although there is today a more obvious blend of cultures in the whole Western world than fifty years ago.

Progress made by Acadians in Nova Scotia and Prince Edward Island has largely revolved around the notion of structures made for them. In New Brunswick the talk has been about "equality" for francophones. Acadians today have more control over their own destiny than they have possessed since 1755. Land remains one of their fundamental values, as was seen when the Vautour family refused to be expelled from Kouchibouguac Park, and during the debate about land for military purposes on the Acadian peninsula.

One loves land all the more after one has lost it. However, younger Acadians are more fond of rock and roll than of haystacks and dried fish. Acadian identity will continue to be a blend of all that has happened in the past. And it is still evolving in many forms.

Acadie today is searching for its direction. It is a dynamic community and thus makes its presence in the Maritimes all the more exciting for all of us.

IV. Economic Challenges

For the Acadians, survival as a community is connected to its distinct linguistic traits and its links with the francophone community in Canada and around the world. And, in its future dealings with the European Community and in its overall cultural and economic development, Canada could enjoy a definite advantage by having a strong French Canadian component, and not only in Quebec. Nova Scotia understood this in 1988 when it organized an official reception for French navy officials, presided over by an Acadian minister, and the province now sends a delegation to the francophone summits that take place every two years. New Brunswick is also increasingly aware of the importance of economic ties with other French-speaking communities, especially at a time when communications networks cross all geographic boundaries and make formerly isolated communities closer to one another day by day.

This is not to say that French Canada should be restricted to links with other French-speaking countries only; nor should Anglo-Canadians be denied access to such networks. Because of its French Canadian component, the whole community can partake of something it could not partake of otherwise, with a distinct advantage over others. Canada can be a privileged partner of at least three major political and economic groups in the world: American, English and French. And Acadians, who have always lived on linguistic borders and have often known two languages, may have a distinct advantage. Both English and French today also mean cultural and economic links with the whole European community.

Anglo-Canadians should realize that Acadians are not simply a group of people who celebrate Evangeline and Gabriel, characters created by an American, once a year during a folk festival, but that they constitute a real society with collective aims, and specific needs in educational, social and economically sustainable development. Acadians are not only folk dancers, musicians and tellers of tales, but also doctors, computer scientists, architects, writers, economists and psychologists. But how can Anglo-Canadians understand that Acadie, after two centuries of silence, has now come back to the point where it can be a real partner and not simply a mere ghost from a romantic past unless Acadians tell them?

V. Preserving Differences in a Planetary Age

One can read several books about Acadian history, yet there is still much to be discovered and written about that history, which is much richer than anyone can conceive, and is now being studied and written about, more and more, by Acadian historians themselves.

One can argue for ages about who was really responsible for the act of war that the English language politely calls the "Expulsion" of the Acadians, and yet the only conclusion one will reach is that, as Annapolis Valley historian Barry Moody puts it: "No simple answers are possible in this complex story." The only clear answer is that the young Acadian community suddenly found itself in a dangerous situation because of events not of its own making. Acadians were never at war with Britain; France was. But discovering, analyzing and rewriting Acadian history would have a very different meaning if the Acadians had not survived.

Some argue that even among Acadians the importance given to the French language is not universal. How could it be, when it has been a constant struggle to preserve that identity and the few traditions that reminded Acadians of where they were coming from and when few historians even bothered to talk about this culture except to mourn its disappearance? Curiously enough, the people who make such pronouncements are rarely Acadians themselves but more often unilingual anglophones trying to justify why they themselves do not make an effort to learn French.

There was much pride in the fact, thanks to Acadian efforts and an intelligent minister of education, that the Clare-Argyle school board worked in French with translation services for its local anglophone minority. What would we say today, when Nova Scotia Acadians have their own school board, with the option at long last of being a francophone community like other minorities in Canada or in Europe? Efforts by French-speaking minorities throughout Canada are not only to have schooling for their own children in their own language, but also to have control over how those schools are managed and how programs are produced. It is the only way to ensure the future of the community as a whole.

Reality for Acadians is not only that France is still a major player in international politics and they can be proud to be among its North American relatives; it is also that Canada is an independent society and neither a copy of Britain nor the United States. In the same way French Canada has its own existence that does nor have to be justified by the existence of France. Acadian groups have had a distinct existence for nearly four centuries.

Bilingualism is simply the recognition that there are in the same space groups whose mother tongue is different, and that such diversity should be recognized by the provision of schooling and a degree of linguistic autonomy to such groups. Acadians can always choose, should they so wish or should their individual destinies lead them to that choice, or in the anglophone world, as a number of them have done and still do. They should, however, not be forced to do so, as they have been in the past.

Being proud to be Acadians and francophone is now officially recognized as being just as important to our Maritime identity as being proud to be of Scottish, Irish, or British origin. The Acadian flag flies over the New Brunswick legislative buildings, it flew over the Nova Scotia legislature for its 100th anniversary, it can be seen by tourists and it is a source of pride among Acadians and Maritimers as a whole. Were this only symbolic, there would be little cause for rejoicing. But concrete steps are being taken, gradually, in favour of Acadians and francophones, and this is cause for rejoicing despite the problems and misunderstandings we still face.

The past cannot be recaptured and changed. The memorial church at Grand-Pré continues to remind us of this. Acadians today face new challenges. Acadie of today, although it may not be a province, and although it may still be far from solutions to all the problems that it inherited, is indeed quite real and has little to do with the romantic tragedy of Evangeline. The most important thing about Acadie today is not the fact that Acadians were expelled and deported. Rather, it is the fact that they survived, came back and claimed what they knew to be their rights, and are now more than ever part of Canada as a growing nation in a planetary age.

Shared difficulties make a community even more aware of its identity, especially when linked with rejection by others. Treated as slaves or cheap labour by New England settlers, Huguenot landowners and Jersey merchants, fiercely Catholic at a time when religion was a major factor of discrimination, Acadians stayed in the Maritimes or came back because this was their land, and they suffered through many humiliations, fights and difficulties to become equal citizens. "What made them survive?" Antonine Maillet was asked a few years ago. "Nothing but themselves," she answered. True, but there was more than a little help from friends, from French instructors like François-Lambert Bourneuf to Father Lefebvre from Quebec, and so many others. This francophone presence in Acadie, which will increase to replace generations not born, is the parallel to immigration from anglophone groups in the Maritimes. It is, both ways, part of our reality.

Religion, language, mottoes from the small Acadian elite and rejection by the English may have helped, but these are only factors added to that fundamental quality of Acadians—tenacity and the will to cling to their land as best they could. The essence of Acadian culture is this will to survive against all odds and to shape their own destiny.

Acadians have created a number of structures to ensure their survival as a national group in the Canadian and Maritime context. Their will, at the end of the nineteenth century, to show the world that their identity was one different from France, from Quebec and from other parts of the world was clearly an indication that they would not accept disappearance into a "melting pot" of some kind.

Whatever else constitutes their identity, what makes Acadians "Acadians" today is their existence as a unique French-speaking group in the Maritimes, ready to accept new immigrants who share that fundamental value with them. Today a spirit of cooperation between all partners in developing francophone realities is more essential and more obvious than ever, but the challenges faced by Acadians are particular to them, and to those immigrants of French, Swiss, Belgian, Haitian, or other origins who have come to live in the diverse francophone space of Acadie.

CHAPTER 6

Some Prominent Individuals

Any selection of individuals from among a community that has a four-century history and has had a good many heroes and heroines and many more dedicated individuals is bound to forget many. There have been many important Acadians, male and female, during the period since the founding of the old Acadie until today in all fields, from farming to business, from the arts to politics, from sports to music. Many have already been mentioned elsewhere in this book. Our aim is to show diversity. Let those who are not included here forgive us.

I. EIGHTEENTH CENTURY

Joseph Broussard, called "Beausoleil," 1702-65

Born at Port-Royal, settled at Le Cran (south of present-day Moncton) in 1740. He was one of the many Acadian fighters during the wars that raged before and after the Expulsion and finally gave himself up in 1758. After 1763 he joined his family in Louisiana. By far the best-known character in the Acadian resistance movement, his name is present in several novels, such as *Pélagie-la-Charrette* by Antonine Maillet, and in the folk-rock music group Beausoleil Broussard, and in the Cajun music group Beausoleil. The Broussard and Beausoleil families keep his memory alive in Acadiana today.

Mathurin Bourg, Missionary, 1744-97

Born near Grand-Pré, he was deported with his family to Virginia (1755) and then to Britain (1756-63). After studying in France, he came back to Canada and became a priest in 1772. Apparently the first priest to have come back to Acadie after the Expulsion, he was a vicar general for Acadian missions from 1774 to 1795.

Mathieu Martin (Sieur de)

Although not quite the first child born in Acadie (although stated by some documents), but possibly the first child educated and raised in Acadie, Mathieu Martin, born at Port-Royal in 1636, received a grant of land from the Marquis de Denonville, Governor of Quebec, on March 29, 1689, which was confirmed by the King of France, Louis XIV on July 14, 1690. The grant covered an important area in the Cobequid area (now Truro), making Mathieu Martin the seignior de Saint-Mathieu. In 1703, there were 87 inhabitants in the seigneurie; in 1714, 128, who decided to stay in Acadie under the Treaty of Utrecht; in 1731, 500. The seigniory was rich farmland, with numerous heads of cattle.

The name of Mathieu Martin has been given to the major high school (polyvalente) in Dieppe, New Brunswick.

II.   NINETEENTH CENTURY

Vénérande Robichaux, 1753-1839

Born at Port-Royal and expelled with her family to Boston in 1755, Vénérande Robichaux came back to Quebec in the 1770s and from then on corresponded steadily with her family in the Miramichi region. Her letters dealing with business questions, political problems, and family matters are among the first important literary documents written by an Acadian about what the community went through during the Expulsion and in the following years, when maintaining a sense of family and community was essential for the future of Acadians between New England, Quebec and the Maritimes. First published in *L'Evangéline* in 1887, her letters were reprinted in the *Revue d'Histoire de la Société Historique Nicolas-Denys*, sept-déc. 1997.

Marcel-François Richard, 1847-1915

Marcel-François Richard is considered by many to be the father of modern Acadie. The ancestors of the Richard family arrived in Acadie from France in 1649, and then moved to New Brunswick following the Expulsion. Joseph Richard, his grandfather, founded Saint-Louis de Kent in 1789. The youngest of ten children, born to a family of modest means, Marcel-François Richard went to study at St. Dunstan's College in Charlottetown following completion of his basic schooling in 1860. He was then able to go to Montreal for studies at the Grand Séminaire. Ordained assistant to the curé of Saint-Louis in

1870, he became curé the same year but faced a long and protracted struggle against his unstable predecessor, which led to the whole population rallying around him in 1874.

In 1874, Richard created Académie Saint-Louis, which he wanted to be a rival to Memramcook's Collège Saint-Joseph. Conflicts with Bishop Rogers, who found the college too nationalistic, led to its closing in 1882. In 1885 he went to Rogersville, a parish he had helped to found in 1870. He devoted his life to building churches, schools and convents throughout Kent and Northumberland counties. He was instrumental in the choice of National Acadian Day (August 15), the Acadian National Hymn ("Ave Maris Stella") and the Acadian flag.

Pascal Poirier, 1852-1933

Born in Shédiac, where his birthplace is now an historic house, Pascal Poirier was named postmaster of the House of Commons at the age of 20 while a student at Collège Saint-Joseph. He completed his law studies at Ottawa and was named a senator in 1885 by Sir John A. Macdonald, to represent Acadian interests particularly. An ardent nationalist, he was among the founders of Société Nationale l'Assomption in 1881, which he presided over while being in the forefront of the National Acadian Congresses. He also presided over Institut Canadien-Français at Ottawa in 1882-83. He was a major fighter in the cause for an Acadian bishop and in most Acadian developments of the late nineteenth and early twentieth centuries. He wrote a number of volumes on Acadian life and history, the best remembered being his linguistic studies, *Le Parler franco-acadien et ses origines* and *Glossaire Acadien*, in which he shows that Acadian French is a form of French close to what was spoken and written in western France in the seventeenth and eighteenth centuries and not a bastardized popular language.

Senator Pascal Poirier, linguist and historian.

Emilie Leblanc, called "Marichette," 1863-1935

Born in Memramcook, Emilie Leblanc studied at the teachers' college in Fredericton and taught in Weymouth, Nova Scotia, for ten years. Between February 14, 1895, and February 3, 1898, she published a number of letters in *L'Evangéline* which are among the first documents written in Acadian French about contemporary topics, from politics to sex, from education and language to the need for women to vote, which she was among the first to advocate for Acadians.

III. TWENTIETH CENTURY

Albert Sormany, 1885-1970

After studies at Laval, this Lamèque native practiced medicine in Edmundston, specializing in radiology. Albert Sormany was among the founders of the weekly *Le Madawaska* in 1913, president of the Société Mutuelle l'Assomption from 1927 to 1951, among the founders of the Collège Saint-Louis and involved in Association Canadienne des Jeunesses Catholiques and Club Richelieu. In 1936 he became the first president of the Association Canadienne d'éducation du Nouveau-Brunswick.

Marguerite Michaud, 1903-82

The first Acadian woman to receive a B.A. (in 1923), Marguerite Michaud obtained her Ph.D. from Université de Montréal in 1947. In-volved with Unesco in 1952 and with the Canadian commission on multi-culturalism in 1975, she wrote several books on the French fact in New Brunswick while teaching at Saint Thomas University in Fredericton (1968-73). She received, among other honours, the Order of Canada.

Arthur Leblanc, 1906-85

Born in Saint-Anselme, Arthur Leblanc followed a family initiation into the world of music with his own studies in Quebec, Boston and Paris. First violin in the Paris symphony (1935-36), he returned to Canada to teach and perform, primarily on radio and television. He created several works, including a "Petite suite canadienne" for piano and violin. As the best known of several Acadians who distinguished themselves in classical music, his name was given to the quartet-in-residence at Université de Moncton in the 1980s. A movie, *Le violon d'Arthur Leblanc*, was the first film produced in 1991 by Les Produc-tions du Fado in Moncton.

Marguerite Michaud *Gilbert Finn*

Gilbert Finn, 1920-

Born in 1920 at Inkerman, New Brunswick, Gilbert Finn studied at Université Laval before a career with the insurance company L'Assomption, where he became president of the board and principal manager in 1969. From 1980 to 1985 he was president of Université de Moncton. Active in many organizations in the Acadian community of Moncton, he was involved in the economic development of the Maritimes with Maritime councils and Acadian economic boards. He was later appointed Lieutenant-Governor of New Brunswick.

Mgr. Robichaud, 1905-79

Ordained a priest in 1931, this native of Saint-Charles-de Kent and former student of Collège Sainte-Anne worked with Monsignor Chiasson in Chatham and Bathurst, becoming a bishop himself in 1942, and the archbishop of Moncton, a position he held until 1972. He led a fundraising campaign in 1943 to support the daily *L'Evangéline* and was honoured by the Conseil de la Vie Française en Amérique for his services to the Acadian community.

Clément Cormier, 1910-1987

Born in Moncton, Clément Cormier became a priest in 1936 and came back to Université Saint-Joseph in 1940, becoming its president in 1948. The first president of the Acadian Université de Moncton in 1963, he worked to promote the French-Acadian reality in all fields— Senate seats for Acadians, creation of a regional network of Radio-Canada in French for the Maritimes, creation of schools and the establishment of an historic Acadian village. He was chancellor of Université de Moncton from 1973 to 1978.

Anselme Chiasson, 1911-

Born in Chéticamp, Cape Breton in 1911, and a Capuchin priest after 1938, Anselme Chiasson acted as a professor and administrator for his order in Ottawa before coming to Moncton in the 1950s. He was instrumental in the development of Société Historique Acadienne, created to preserve and promote Acadian history, and in the founding of Centre d'Etudes Acadiennes at Université de Moncton, which is the main repository of Acadian archives. He acted as its first director. Among his many books is *Chéticamp, histoire et traditions acadiennes*, published in 1969. Considered a major milestone in the study of local communities within the broader picture of Acadian history, society and culture, it was translated into English. Chiasson collaborated on many historical and folklore studies (in particular on the Magdalen Islands) and archival projects and his volumes of Acadian songs are still the major source of material for those who sing them. He received honorary degrees from the Acadian universities of Moncton and Sainte-Anne, the Order of Canada, and the Palmes Académiques from the government of France.

Léger Comeau, 1920-1997

Born in 1920 at Saulnierville, Nova Scotia, Léger Comeau studied in Rome and Montreal before teaching in Edmundston, Bathurst, Halifax and at Université Sainte-Anne, where he became vice-president of external relations in 1986. Involved in many local and regional organizations, he founded Fédération Acadienne de la Nouvelle-Ecosse in 1967 and acted as its president from 1967 to 1969 and 1978 to 1982. In 1978 he became the president of Société Nationale des Acadiens and for a decade was an active ambassador of Acadians

Léger Comeau.

throughout Canada and in France. He received many awards and honours, including the Prix Séraphin Marion from Société Saint-Jean Baptiste in Montreal, and the Légion d'Honneur given by French president François Mitterand. He died in 1997, receiving the honours of a national funeral from the whole of Acadie.

Martin Légère, 1916-

Martin Légère was born in 1916. After studying at St. Francis Xavier and at Laval, he pursued a career in the Caisses Populaires Acadiennes. From 1942 to 1982 he was general manager of Fédération des Caisses Populaires and of the complementary insurance system. He also acted as secretary of Conseil Acadien de la Coopération while working with other Canadian institutions, and international organizations such as Alliance Coopérative Internationale. President of the society publishing the daily *L'Evangéline* from 1950 to 1981, he carried on his interests in newspaper publishing as president of Les Oeuvres de Presse Acadienne (1980-82). Holder of several honorary degrees and an officer of the Order of Canada, he is considered a major figure in the Caraquet area of New Brunswick.

Muriel Roy, 1921-

Born in 1921 and trained at Université de Montréal, Muriel Roy taught sociology and demography at Université de Moncton from 1971 to 1982. She chaired a 1981 commission to find a solution to the Kouchibouguac Park problem and has been active on many committees, for Parks Canada in particular, devoting attention to see that the needs of Acadians are served by that federal organization. In 1982 she became director of Centre d'Etudes Acadiennes. Her little volume, *Les Acadiens*, co-authored with French sociologist Jean-William Lapierre, has received wide recognition.

Gérard LaForest, 1926-

Born in Grand Falls, New Brunswick in 1926, Gérard LaForest became a lawyer in 1949, after finishing his studies at Yale and Oxford. Professor of law at the University of New Brunswick from 1956 to 1968, he was dean of the law faculty at the University of Alberta from 1968 to 1970. A specialist in constitutional law and a member of the Canada Law Reform Commission, he became Appeals Court Judge for New Brunswick in 1981, before becoming a member of the Supreme Court of Canada.

Louis-Joseph Robichaud, 1925-

The "Robichaud era" in Acadian History is similar to the "Revolution tranquille" (Quiet Revolution) in Quebec's history. Born in 1925, this young lawyer from Saint-Antoine, studied in Bathurst and Quebec before being admitted to the bar and beginning his political career in

Louis-Joseph Robichaud.

1952. In 1959 he became leader of the opposition, and in 1960 premier of New Brunswick. He fought for equality between the two main linguistic groups in that province, and for regional development to counteract disparities. His name is closely associated with the founding of Université de Moncton and with the official New Brunswick languages Act. Defeated in 1971, he became a senator in Ottawa in 1973. The movie *Robichaud* by Herménégilde Chiasson recognized how much New Brunswick Acadians owe him.

Antonine Maillet, major Acadian writer.

Antonine Maillet, 1929-

Born in 1929, this Bouctouche native has become, for many, synonymous with Acadie. After studies in Moncton, Montreal, Quebec City and Paris, including a Ph.D. from Laval (1970), and a number of years as a teacher in New Brunswick schools and universities, she has written many successful plays, including *La Sagouine* in the 1970s, *Gapi et Sullivan, La Contrebandière* and many others. She is best known internationally for her novels, having been, with *Pélagie-la-Charette* (1979), the first French Canadian author by birth to win the Prix Concourt, the top literary award in France. She has written about ten other novels, including *MariaaGélas* (1973), *Crache-à-Pic* and *L'Oursiade* (1990). She has been honoured by scores of universities, has won many awards and was named chancellor of Université de Moncton. She represents Canada on many international boards, in particular the Haut Conseil de la Francophonie in Paris.

Viola Léger, 1930-

Born in 1930 in Massachusetts, Viola Léger studied fine arts at Boston University before teaching in New Brunswick schools. In 1971 her friend Antonine Maillet asked her to interpret the role of *La Sagouine* in the play by that name, and she made it into an international success, performing it more than 700 times. In the 1970s she returned to New Brunswick after having performed mostly in Quebec and created her own company, showing her many talents in plays and movies such as *Harold and Maude* and *Cap-Lumière*. She has received many awards, including the Prix Méritas in 1990 given by Fédération Acadienne du Québec.

Claude Roussel, 1930-

Born in 1930, after studying in Montreal, this Edmundston native came back to teach fine arts in Moncton, opening new territory in Acadian culture and society. He founded, among other things, the art gallery and fine arts department of Université de Moncton, and his sculptures have won national and international recognition for their continually innovative techniques. He was named to the Order of Canada in 1982 and Les Éditions d'Acadie published a book for the occasion, recognizing the importance of his work.

MARTINE JACQUOT

Claude Roussel.

Melvin Gallant.

Melvin Gallant, 1932-

Born on Prince Edward Island in 1932, Melvin Gallant returned to Acadie after completing a Ph.D. in Switzerland and started teaching French and Acadian literature at Moncton in 1964. Although most of his books have documentary value, such as the texts and photos of *Le Pays d'Acadie* or the recipes he co-authored in *La Cuisine traditionnelle en Acadie*, he was recognized as a novelist and received the France-Acadie award for *Le Chant des Grenouilles* (1982). He was a driving force behind the creation in 1972 of Les Éditions d'Acadie, the first Acadian publisher in the Maritimes, and the team that produced *Les Maritimes: trois provinces à découvrir*, one of the first social sciences textbooks ever produced regionally for Acadian schools. His Acadian tale, *Ti-Jean* (1973), was one of the first books read in New Brunswick schools. He has written poetry and scholarly articles and is the founder or co-founder of several organizations, including Association des Ecrivains Acadiens and Société Egalité, a political think tank for the future of Acadians. Melvin Gallant is now living and writing full-time from his home in the Dominican Republic, after a few years in Martinique.

Muriel Roy   Michel Bastarache

Edith Butler, 1942-

Edith Butler was born in 1942. From Paquetville, she graduated with a B.A. from Université de Moncton in 1964, already well known then as an interpreter of Acadian folklore. The 1970s saw her reach a much larger audience with a variety of songs, and several of her LPs were well received in France and Canada. Her recitals at L'Olympia in Paris were a huge success. Her dynamic attitude, powerful voice and rich knowledge of Acadian songs with modern musical accompaniments make her by far the best known Acadian popular artist. She has consistently helped Acadian artists in other fields and has received several awards, including the Order of Canada, and the Order of Merit from the government of France.

Michel Bastarache, 1947-

Born in 1947 at Quebec City, Michel Bastarache obtained a B.A. at Université de Moncton, a law degree from Université de Montréal, a DES in public law from Université de Nice (France) and a Bachelor in Common Law from the University of Ottawa. Having worked as a law translator (1970), he became executive director of the Société

Nationale des Acadiens (1973), then moved up to the vice-presidency of Insurance l'Assomption in 1977. He became its president in 1989, after having been law professor and dean of law at Université de Moncton (1978-83), working as director of promotion for official languages with the Secretary of State of Canada (1983-84) and associate dean of law at the University of Ottawa (after 1984). He has been a major consultant for the development of common law programs in French and, besides many activities in the scholarly field in law and political science, has been co-chair of the controversial Poirier-Bastarache commission (1981) which recommended specific language policies throughout New Brunswick to satisfy Acadian rights in that province. His nomination by Prime Minister Jean Chrétien to the Supreme Court of Canada in 1997 was the crowning recognition of the fact that Acadians have developed high expertise in the legal field, particularly in all that relates to questions of national policy in Canada.

Claude Bourque, 1945-

Born in 1945 in Moncton, Claude Bourque has a B.A. from Université de Moncton and a journalism degree from Université de Strasbourg (France) After having been legislative correspondent in Fredericton for *L'Evangéline* (1967-68), the assistant director for information services of New Brunswick (1969-71) and then chief editor of *L'Evangéline* (1971-77), he moved to electronic media, becoming director of French services for Radio-Canada in the Atlantic region in 1982.

Herménégilde Chiasson, 1946-

Born in 1946 at Saint-Simon in northern New Brunswick, Herménégilde Chiasson studied at Collège Saint-Joseph, Université de Moncton, and Mount Allison University, completing his studies at Rochester, New York, and later received a Ph.D. from La Sorbonne in Paris. A visual artist exhibiting regularly, he became known as a major Acadian poet in the 1970s, with *Mourir à Scoudouc* in 1974, *Rapport sur l'Etat de mes illusions* in 1976 and *Prophéties* in 1986. Having worked for Radio-Canada, he became interested in filmmaking in the 1980s. His movies on Jack Kerouac (*Le Grand Jack*), Madame LaTour, and Louis Robichaud in particular, have attracted public interest and won him praise. He was the recipient in 1990 of the Order of Arts and Letters given by the government of France for significant artistic achievements.

Herménégilde Chiasson.

Roméo LeBlanc (the Rt. Hon.)

The Right Honourable Roméo LeBlanc, Governor General and Commander-in-Chief of Canada, was born in Memramcook (L'Anse-Aux-Cormier), New Brunswick, in 1927. He had a successful career as a teacher, a journalist, and a major political figure in the Liberal party of Canada.

Educated at Université St-Joseph (B.A., 1984; B.Ed., 1951), he started teaching at Drummond High School, New Brunswick (1951-1953) and at the New Brunswick Teachers College, Fredericton (1955-1959), after studying French civilization at l'Université de Paris from 1953 to 1955.

He turned to journalism and became a correspondent for Radio-

Canada in Ottawa (1960-1962), the United Kingdom (1962-1965) and the United States (1965-1967). In 1965, he was Founding President of the CBC/Radio-Canada Correspondents' Association. He served as Press Secretary to Prime Ministers Lester B. Pearson (1967-1968) and Pierre Elliott Trudeau (1968-1971), and Director of Public Relations at l'Université de Moncton (1971-1972).

First elected to the House of Commons in 1972, representing Westmorland-Kent, he served for ten years as a Minister of the Crown: Fisheries (1974-1976), Fisheries and the Environment (1976-1979), Fisheries and Oceans (1980-1982), Public Works (1982-1984), making official visits to the USSR, Poland, Cuba, the EEC, the United Kingdom and France. Member of the delegation to the United Nations Law of the Sea Conference from 1974 to 1979, he chaired, among other cabinet committees, the Communications committee (1974-1984). He became a Senator on June 29, 1984. An active member of the Canada-France Parliamentary Association and the International Association of French-speaking Parliamentarians (AIPLF), he served on numerous Senate committees before being appointed Speaker of the Senate on December 7, 1993.

Appointed Governor General of Canada on November 22, 1994, he was sworn into office on February 8, 1995. Through his appointment, the Acadian star is now among the official symbols of Canada.

A Visiting Scholar at the Institute of Canadian Studies, Carleton University, Ottawa (1985-86), part-time Faculty Member, Canadian Studies, at Concordia University in Montreal, he has received honorary degrees from Mount Allison University (1977), the Université de Moncton (1979), and Université Sainte-Anne, Nova Scotia (1995).

Mr. LeBlanc is married to Diana Fowler, originally from Ontario, who herself had a rich career in journalism and social work. They have four children.

AUTHOR'S ACKNOWLEDGEMENTS

The song by Donat Lacroix, "Viens voir l'Acadie" is copyrighted with Editions Gabriel-CAPAC. This translation © Henri-Dominique Paratte. The quotation by Captain Vaudron as translated here is excerpted from M.A. MacDonald, *Fortune and La Tour,* Methuen, 1983, p.129. The quotation from Michel Antoine is from Louis XV (Paris: Fayard, 1989), p.671. Original translation © H-D. Paratte. The translated quotation from Jean-Claude Vemex, *Les Acadiens*, Editions Entente, 1979, was first used in "Echos d'Acadie," texts and photographs, 1980, © H-D Paratte and Geneviève Houêt. The paragraph translated from *Les Portes Tournantes*, by Jacques Savoie, is from p.45 of the 1984 Boréal Express edition. Translation © H-D Paratte. Excerpt from Frederick Cozzens is from *Acadia*, original edition (New York: Derby and Nassau, 1859), pp.39-40. Quotation by Brian Mulroney is from *Where I Stand* (Toronto: McLelland and Stewart, 1983), p.94. Quotation from Robert Darnton is from *The Great Cat Massacre* (and other episodes in French Cultural History), Basic Books, 1984, p.29. Quotation from Janice Kulyk Keefer is from *Constellations*, 1988, p.3. Quotation from Antonine Maillet's *La Sagouine* is translated by Luis de Cespedes.

INDEX

Thibault, Charelle 192
Thibodeau, Eléonore 99
Thibodeau, Félix 143, 155
Thibodeau, Pierre 31
Thibodeaux, Ambroise 118
Third Republic 11
Tignish 56, 63
Tignish convention 1913 63
Trappist Monks 113
Tricoche, Georges Nestler 114
Trudeau, Pierre 91

union of three provinces 66
Université de Moncton 115, 133, 159
Université Sainte-Anne 115, 133, 159
Université Saint-Joseph 86
Utrecht, treaty of 38

Valcourt, Bernard 95, 106
Vanheck, Yvan 161
Vaughan, Betty Boudreau 162
veillées 159
Veniot, Pierre-Jean 69, 93
verb forms 127
Vienne region 15
Villebon, Governor 32
Vincent, Father 113 .
Visages de Femmes 100
visual art 164-165
Voisine, Roch 106, 116, 139

Wedgeport 150
West Pubnico 150
Williams, Katharine Reid 48, 162
Windsor 37
wines 32
women 51
women, groups 100
women, vote 52, 99
women, symbols 104
women, traditional activities 100
writers, anglophone 162

Young, Doug 98

Zéro Degré Celsius 135